Planning Our
Future Libraries

Planning Our Future Libraries

Blueprints for 2025

Kim Leeder &
Eric Frierson

Editors

An Imprint of the American Library Association
Chicago   2014

Kim Leeder is director of library services at the College of Western Idaho and a co-founder of *In the Library with the Lead Pipe*. Since earning her master's degree in information resources and library science at the University of Arizona in 2006, she has worked in reference, instruction, and administration at several academic and public libraries. Leeder has been recognized as an ALA Emerging Leader (2008) and a *Library Journal* Mover and Shaker (2011). She is actively involved in the American Library Association and the Association of College and Research Libraries.

Eric Frierson is a Discovery Services Engineer at EBSCO Publishing. He is formerly the head of Library Systems at St. Edward's University library, a reference and instruction librarian at the University of Texas at Arlington, and an instructional technology librarian at the University of Michigan. Frierson holds a Master of Science in Information from the University of Michigan and a bachelor's degree in computer science and English, and is a former high school teacher. His interest in library leadership stems from participation in Texas Library Association's TALL Texans program and the American Library Association's Emerging Leaders program.

Printed in the United States of America
18 17 16 15 14   5 4 3 2 1

Extensive effort has gone into ensuring the reliability of the information in this book; however, the publisher makes no warranty, express or implied, with respect to the material contained herein.

ISBN: 978-0-8389-1207-2 (paper) — PDF ISBN: 978-0-8389-9686-7
ePub ISBN: 978-0-8389-9688-1 — Kindle ISBN: 978-0-8389-9687-4

Library of Congress Cataloging-in-Publication Data

Planning our future libraries : blueprints for 2025 / Kim Leeder, Eric Frierson, editors.
      pages   cm
   Includes bibliographical references and index.
   ISBN 978-0-8389-1207-2 (alk. paper)
1. Library planning.   2. Libraries—Forecasting.   3. Public services (Libraries)—Forecasting.
4. Organizational change.   I. Leeder, Kim., editor of compilation.   II. Frierson, Eric, editor of compilation.
   Z678.P575 2014   11/14   5498 7069
   022'.3—dc23   2013028246

Cover design by Kimberly Thornton. Images © Shutterstock, Inc.
Text design and composition in the Gotham and Charis SIL typefaces by Scribe Inc.

♾ This paper meets the requirements of ANSI/NISO Z39.48-1992 (Permanence of Paper).

Contents

Introduction

This is not the first book to attempt to forecast the future of libraries, nor will it be the last. The rapid pace of change in librarianship over the past 30 years has created an environment of instability that many are eager to dispel. If nature abhors a vacuum, librarians detest the uncertainty of the future—and with good reason. Libraries throughout the United States have seen their budgets slashed, branches closed, and missions challenged. The short-term economic forecast offers little promise of a reversal. Without some concrete vision through which to redefine their form and function, it appears possible, even likely, that libraries could soon be headed into oblivion.

Those prepared to wail and gnash their teeth in distress, however, can take heart in the pages of this book. The institution of libraries has been challenged before, as described in Brett Bonfield's opening chapter, "Redesigning Library Services Again." Bonfield sets the context for the subsequent chapters by revisiting Michael Buckland's 1992 work of forecasting, *Redesigning Library Services: A Manifesto*, an abridged version of which is available as an appendix to this book. Buckland's treatise sets its foundation, as does *Planning Our Future Libraries: Blueprints for 2025*, on the "first principles" of librarianship. In order to assess the effectiveness of libraries, as he points out, it is first necessary to reevaluate the structure that supports them. Regardless of changes in culture or technology, the first principles of librarianship remain deeply rooted in the "Library Bill of Rights," which has been updated but not significantly altered since it was originally drafted in 1939 (American Library Association 1996). Libraries in the United States and beyond continue to champion intellectual freedom, pursue equitable access to information, and challenge censorship, no matter what platform hosts the information at hand.

With the grounding of librarianship's first principles, it becomes possible to project more objectively and constructively into the future. To that end, *Planning Our Future Libraries: Blueprints for 2025* brings together eight new voices in librarianship whose fresh, unvarnished visions portray a near-term library future that leverages current strengths to evolve and expand the role of libraries in the twenty-first century. By focusing on the most relevant and innovative qualities of today's libraries and librarians, the authors included here share their unique yet overlapping predictions of where libraries are, or should be, headed. Together they construct a solid, inspiring, and entirely achievable future library toward which the field can advance.

While each chapter in *Planning Our Future Libraries: Blueprints for 2025* stands on its own, a collective reading of the full book reveals several overarching themes that serve as its organizing structure. First, the opening two chapters highlight the importance of patron participation as a key characteristic of a successful future library. Second, chapters 3 through 5 tackle the challenge of reimagining libraries' physical spaces, both in terms of how library buildings might be designed and how library spaces can be reconceived. Chapters 6 and 7 present new ways to reinvent library function and infrastructure through an innovative model of staff time allocation and a proposal to increase and stabilize library funding. Finally, in chapter 8, Lesley Farmer steps beyond these themes to provide an assessment of the current and future state of international libraries in developing nations.

Embracing Participation

The history of libraries is a history of control; until recently, librarians controlled the selection, organization, description, and provision of access to the great majority of information. With the Internet, of course, that control has leaked gradually out of libraries and into the hands of the public. The "Library 2.0" movement that began in the early 2000s, whose origin is attributed to Michael Casey of LibraryCrunch (Casey and Savastinuk 2007), has begun to give way to the broader concept of the "Participatory Library." In the Participatory Library, patrons are invited and empowered to join librarians and library staff in shaping the library to meet their needs. Barbara Fister (2012) recently defined the Participatory Library as an effort to make libraries "a platform for creating and sharing culture."

The first two chapters of *Planning Our Future Libraries: Blueprints for 2025* emphasize the role that patrons play in sustaining the library. In fact, Bonfield suggests that the terms "patron" and "user" don't accurately describe how people will interact with libraries in 2025 and instead considers the term "member" to more accurately reflect the relationship between people and libraries. Librarians and library members, he suggests, will cocreate the new library through conversation, brainstorming, and feedback. In Bonfield's vision of the Participatory Library, the library responds not just to what library members need from the library but to what they need in *life*. Through conversation, members and librarians draw upon a shared pool of knowledge and experience to ensure that the library will succeed. In this scenario, patron-driven acquisitions, aided by widely adopted standards and easy-to-use licensing, become a powerful tool that members use to design their own library collections. Acquisitions also serve as a platform for members to share experiences in person and virtually. The Participatory Library is filled with thinkers, readers, makers, and doers, and it provides the tools and the environment for all to flourish.

Dave Harmeyer, in "Radical Trust: A User-Librarian Shared Model," presents the notion of "radical trust" as a characteristic of libraries that include the people they serve in library decision making. He argues that a transition to the Participatory Library is vital, as it addresses several key challenges that threaten the sustainability of libraries. Because user needs are changing too rapidly for libraries to accommodate, increased member participation enables a library to be more nimble and responsive to the community it serves. In his vision, the library provides avenues for members to engage in planning activities and to set priorities for the library. Harmeyer anticipates that by relinquishing total control of library decision making, librarians will become part of the creation of something entirely more useful: a library that truly reflects the needs of its community and adapts quickly as those needs change. According to Harmeyer, participation and trust extend to all aspects of the library, and what results is a living, growing, and changing organization that remains in sync with its environment.

Reimagining Spaces

The promise of the Participatory Library lies in adopting new roles and services that address member needs. But what about long-entrenched services that no longer serve the community as they once did, such as legacy book collections? In chapter 3, "Meaningful Space in a Digital Age," Ben Malczewski shares his own reaction to the disappearance of DVDs, print books, and other tangible materials found in a library: *Wait, that's my stuff!* In his chapter, Malczewski explores the psychological and symbolic meaning of the physical spaces and tangible materials in libraries. Even if all of our content can be accessed via the Internet, will it satisfy us to have a library without codex-lined shelves? He argues that while content can be converted to digital formats, the physical objects provide a sense of place and of self. Furthermore, a library as a collection of physical materials evokes intelligence, research, and reflective thought. Malczewski argues that a computing facility with a robust online collection may not lose *content*, but it certainly loses symbolic value. Meaningful spaces can still be created in a bookless library, however. Malczewski makes the case for "narrative design" in the planning of library space. He encourages consideration of the stories patrons bring to a space: What did they come there to do? Who did they encounter? Were they comfortable studying there? It is possible, he projects, to design spaces that inspire positive stories. At that point, removing the stacks becomes liberating instead of frightening.

Krisellen Maloney's chapter on the Faculty Commons tackles this challenge. In her vision, the library is a "platform for faculty innovation" that encourages activity by providing the resources required for collaborative work: technology-enriched workspaces, services attuned to the research and teaching needs of a university faculty, and events that draw people together to engage in creative conversation. This library is a new kind of center for faculty life, providing a compelling narrative for the faculty experience. So how do libraries make this vibrant environment a reality? Maloney draws upon the history of library buildings in order to anticipate the obstacles and opportunities that will arise in moving toward this vision. Similar shifts in library space planning have happened before, only to be undone by library staff who struggled to reinvent their identity in the wake of changing user needs. *The solution is a shift from inward thinking to outward thinking.* Rather than designing libraries to meet staff needs, Maloney asserts, librarians should design spaces to meet *community* needs.

To Hugh Rundle, author of chapter 5, "Free-Range Librarianship," physical library spaces only limit the ability of librarians to serve patron needs. He views information as an environment that humans inhabit, equivalent to the natural world. In his vision, librarians serve as expert guides who support and assist those seeking information, much as park rangers work with visitors to national parks. Like a park ranger who roams the park and provides on-demand assistance to hikers on the trail, the librarian travels throughout the information environment, working in coffee shops, visiting local businesses, attending city hall meetings, and checking in anywhere that information needs are likely to arise. In this model, the library space is *everywhere*. Rundle flips the concept of embedded librarianship upside down, viewing the physical library as unnecessary to the work of a librarian. Like park rangers, librarians are visible in the communities they serve, provide in-context assistance, and most importantly, show up in these spaces in person.

Building New Infrastructure

The visions presented in *Planning Our Future Libraries: Blueprints for 2025* are far removed from the current state of libraries. They present a compelling vision of what libraries can become, but to get there, significant changes are needed in the day-to-day internal workings of these organizations. "[A] library will not be able to innovate if management is not willing to invest time in research and development," writes Meredith Farkas (2010, 36). "If you want to create new services and employ new technologies for your patrons, something has to give." The status quo cannot persist: library administrators will be challenged to develop a positive culture that encourages future-focused change while still grappling with existing financial and cultural challenges. Chapters 6 and 7 of *Planning Our Future Libraries: Blueprints for 2025* present concrete strategies that will change library infrastructure—specifically in terms of budgets and allocation of staff time—and enable the advancement of libraries.

For libraries to effect the sort of change necessary for future success, staff must be encouraged and supported in efforts to reinvent spaces, services, and resources. In chapter 6, "The Constant Innovator," Megan Hodge envisions a profession characterized by constant innovation and creation. Rather than relying on vendors and other outside organizations, librarians take the reins to redesign their own systems. Giving up vendor solutions and adopting open source products will require new sets of skills, and Hodge advocates new management practices to foster such skill development. She cites Google's "20 percent time" as a management strategy that will allow library staff to explore, learn, create, and effect change. The 20 percent time model provides employees with a significant number of work hours—ideally 20 percent of their total hours each week—to devote to unstructured, unregulated innovation. Hodge's chapter describes some practical management strategies for developing a culture of constant innovation, paving the way for immediate changes to take place in our organizations.

The greatest innovations in the world alone, however, are not enough to sustain libraries. Libraries in general—and public libraries in particular—will also need a new funding model that ends their reliance on the mood of local governments by stabilizing and expanding their financial support. In chapter 7, "The Future of Funding," John Chrastka suggests methods through which libraries across the United States can work together to solve their financial woes. By uniting libraries and strategically positioning them as a group to benefit from the US tax code, Social Impact Bonds, and a national trust, the library of 2025 will enjoy reliable, even generous funding to support new services and initiatives.

Leading for the Future

In the introduction to *Shaping the Future: Advancing the Understanding of Leadership*, Peter Hernon (2010) defines leaders as those who set a vision and can influence others to move toward it. Clearly, the authors of *Planning Our Future Libraries: Blueprints for 2025* possess the skills, knowledge, and passion required to lead our institutions toward the bold futures they envision. It will not be a revised mission statement or a well-written vision statement that will spark change, but rather it will be the leaders in the library field who have both a sense of purpose and the ability to motivate action. Library leaders are charged not only with creating a vision for the future of libraries but also with inspiring and motivating everyone in their organizations to make those visions reality.

So what does the future hold for the library profession? That depends on what today's librarians and library leaders make of it. It is entirely within their power to realize a library of the future that is participatory, responsive, reimagined, and flexible, as envisioned within the pages of this book. *Planning Our Future Libraries: Blueprints for 2025* is intended to be more than just a book; it is a challenge and an inspiration to everyone working toward a more positive future for libraries. The editors hope that the visions presented here will serve as a springboard for discussion at libraries around the country and world. Readers are invited to ask themselves the following: How will the Participatory Library function in my community? What will my future library look like physically? How will my library adjust its management and funding models to support innovation and future change? These are complex and important questions, whose answers become substantially clearer thanks to the diverse and creative ideas presented in the following pages.

Reinventing libraries in the twenty-first century will not be easy; however, it has been done before—successfully—and it will be done again. The key is to keep in mind that libraries are not buildings or legacy book collections, but rather a cultural institution that champions free and full access to information for all. The platforms through which that information is obtained, the spaces in which people obtain it, and the services that support their activities are only the details of their function. The details will always evolve to meet the needs of the community. Regardless of shifts in technology and culture, however, the meaning of libraries is and will always be a constant that ensures their ongoing value in a changing world.

References

American Library Association. 1996. "The Library Bill of Rights." www.ala.org/advocacy/intfreedom/librarybill.

Buckland, Michael K. 1992. *Redesigning Library Services: A Manifesto*. Chicago: American Library Association. http://sunsite.berkeley.edu/Literature/Library/Redesigning/html.html.

Casey, Michael E., and Laura C. Savastinuk. 2007. *Library 2.0: A Guide to Participatory Library Service*. Medford, NJ: Information Today.

Farkas, Meredith. 2010. "Technology in Practice. Nurturing Innovation: Tips for Managers and Administrators." *American Libraries* 41, no. 10: 36.

Fister, Barbara. 2012. "Participatory Culture, Participatory Libraries." *Inside Higher Ed* (blog), August 14 (10:49 p.m.). www.insidehighered.com/blogs/library-babel-fish/participatory-culture-participatory-libraries.

Hernon, Peter. 2010. *Shaping the Future: Advancing the Understanding of Leadership.* Santa Barbara, CA: Libraries Unlimited.

Part 1

Embracing Participation

Chapter 1

REDESIGNING LIBRARY SERVICES AGAIN

Revisiting Buckland's Manifesto

Brett Bonfield

"Any attempt to explain the past and to predict the future is foolhardy," writes Michael Buckland (1992, x) in the introduction to *Redesigning Library Services: A Manifesto*. "In this case the importance of the issues seemed worth the effort and the risk." Fortunately, the two decades since the American Library Association released this 82-page monograph have justified both Buckland's effort and his risk. For example, I saw Karen Calhoun (2006a, 2006b) present on "The Catalog's Future" in November 2006, just a few months after she released "The Changing Nature of the Catalog and Its Integration with Other Discovery Tools," her controversial study on this same topic for the Library of Congress. After her presentation, I asked her what library-related texts she considered her major influences. "Have you read Buckland's *Manifesto*?" she asked. "That's the one work I find myself going back to over and over again." Here is another bit of evidence regarding the esteem in which Buckland's work is held: as of August 2012, 778 WorldCat libraries held a copy of *Redesigning Library Services: A Manifesto*, even though it was out of print by 1996 and subsequently made available for free online.

Buckland's manifesto, an abridged version of which is available as an appendix to this book, was the realization of 10 years of research and reflection (1992, x). The idea was to encapsulate the knowledge and beliefs that he had developed over the previous decade in order to help others plan for the *next* 10 years of library services. We have a similar goal for *Planning Our Future Libraries: Blueprints for 2025*, though the editors have chosen writers who are somewhat newer to the profession than Buckland was at the time. He began his career at Bodleian Library of Oxford University, where he was a student. After graduating and earning a library degree at Sheffield University, he was hired for his first professional position at the University of Lancaster Library in 1965. He completed his PhD at Sheffield University in 1972, the same year he moved to the United States to take a job as Assistant Director of Libraries for Technical Services at Purdue University. A few years later, he was hired by the University of California, Berkeley, and served as Dean of the School of Library and Information Studies from 1976 until 1984; then he spent 1983 through 1987 serving as Assistant Vice President for Library Plans and Policies for the University of California's nine campuses ("Michael Buckland," n.d.). His goal, both for the University of California and subsequently for *Redesigning Library Services*, was to plan appropriately for the needs of library users and librarians, and for how their interests seemed most likely to intersect with forthcoming changes in technology and culture.

This chapter, in addition to summarizing Buckland's research and evaluating his predictions, mirrors the structure of *Redesigning Library Services*. Buckland looked to the past to help him predict the future, devoting about half his manifesto to a summary of his research into earlier efforts to shape the library of the future. He found that his predecessors in the field had successfully predicted many of the technologies and services that were being instituted at the time he wrote his manifesto, placing his effort into a continuum and providing him with a sensible way to approach his task. Using Buckland's research and ideas as a platform, this chapter takes a similar approach, with a goal of offering useful suggestions about the library in 2025.

Buckland's Assumption and Three Types of Libraries

Buckland (1992) based his manifesto on five assumptions, one of which is particularly useful for our purpose. In the introduction, he writes, "[D]isproportionate attention has been paid to new information technology" (2). It is not that too much attention has been paid to computing, data storage, and telecommunications, but rather that too little critical attention has been paid to the older information technologies of paper, card, and microfilm. Some of his assumptions are intentionally obvious, serving as points of departure for his more counterintuitive or debatable assertions, but this point is provocative: the idea that new technology is important but not inherently better or more important than old technology. As Buckland emphasizes throughout his book, the goal is not to replace the means through which library services are delivered but to improve upon the ends by creating services that better satisfy users' wants and needs. For the previous 100 years—from the creation of modern libraries in the late nineteenth century through the 1970s—the means and ends were indistinguishable from one another (Buckland 1992, 4). As Buckland was writing his *Manifesto*, newer electronic technologies were making it possible to separate the means from the ends, but he was not in favor of thought-lessly casting aside skills and methods that libraries had spent a century developing. For Buckland, that century of library history was not divided into discrete paradigm shifts; instead, it was divided into a series of three overlapping stages: the Paper Library, the Automated Library, and the Electronic Library.

The Paper Library

During the Paper Library stage of development, which for Buckland comprises roughly the late 1800s through the early 1970s, the library's materials and technical operations were entirely based on paper or other similar materials such as cardboard, vellum, and film. Today, we might call this the Material Library, because Buckland's definition of "paper" could be extended to music CDs, DVD and Blu-ray discs, and even DRM-encoded e-books. That is, they generally require a lot of space to store, typically only one person at a time can use each item, and that person and the item must be in the same place at the same time (Buckland 1992, 10).

Buckland cites numerous examples of pioneering librarians, bibliographers, documentalists, and others who worked in the Paper Library era but understood its limitations and attempted to compensate for them, including the following:

- Paul Otlet and Robert Goldschmidt, who in 1925 envisioned a "pocket-sized" reader for microfilm-based books
- Fritz Donker Duyvis, who in 1931 envisioned the digital circuitry then being developed for telephones as the proper medium for creating devices that could handle complex Boolean and faceted searches
- Walter Schürmeyer, who in 1935 envisioned a time in which readers would access books from their homes through their televisions

For Buckland (1992, 11–14), these pioneers' insights, along with designs by their contemporaries Freemont Rider, Emmanuel Goldberg, Vannevar Bush, and Ralph Shaw, demonstrate that we are capable of looking at the problems we face and the services that would benefit our users, and of describing with considerable precision the solutions that will meet their needs, even if the present technology is not yet able to support these innovations.

The Automated Library

During this stage in library development, spanning roughly from the early 1970s through the 1990s, the library's technical operations were computerized but its collections retained the properties of paper. The primary innovations during the Automated Library period were standards, particularly widespread implementation of Machine-Readable Cataloging (MARC), which "enables computer-based bibliographic data to be shared," and the introduction of Z39.50, which "enables retrieval systems to be shared" (Buckland 1992, 20). This sharing of bibliographic data and the introduction of systems that enabled library operations to be automated were the central innovations of the Automated Library. Buckland specified eight requirements for such a library, including the following:

1. The overall bibliographic coverage should be as complete as possible in providing access to the whole of human knowledge.

2. Multiple access points should be provided, minimally by subject as well as author.

3. It should be a distributed system in that everyone should be able to have access to it and that it should be possible for files to be partitioned and copied for efficiency. . . .

8. The bibliographic system should help to protect intellectual property. (Buckland 1992, 37)

Buckland's requirements reiterate those specified by Henri La Fontaine and Paul Otlet, who developed their Universal Bibliographic Repertory in 1895. The fact that La Fontaine and Otlet, operating at the advent of the Paper Library, could create functional requirements for the Automated Library suggests that Buckland, operating in the Automated Library, could create requirements for the succeeding stage, the Electronic Library. After all, the process of computerizing bibliographic records was similar to the process of computerizing the source material those records described, and in many ways digitizing metadata is more complicated than digitizing source material (Buckland 1992, 47). The design and technology for these projects would require funding and effort, but their realization seemed well within reach. However, Buckland (1992, 40) noted presciently, "It seems likely that conflicting interests between the stakeholders will prove more of a constraint on the development of future library services than narrower questions of design and technology."

The Electronic Library

During this stage in library development, identified as the late 1980s or early 1990s through at least the early 2000s, library operations are electronic and their collections are available in electronic form as well. Today, we refer to Digital or Virtual Libraries to convey this concept. Buckland described several "characteristics of electronic documents," including the following:

1. Electronic documents are not localized. Given telecommunications connections, an electronic document can be used from anywhere, without one even knowing where it is stored geographically.

2. In practice several people can use the same database or electronic records at the same time.

3. Electronic documents are easily copied.

4. Documents stored electronically are very flexible. They are easy to revise, rearrange, reformat, and combine with other documents. Hence the popularity of word-processing among people who have to create and, more especially, revise documents. . . . (Buckland 1992, 43)

Support for these electronic documents required a new kind of approach to library service and a more robust technical infrastructure. Based on the characteristics above, Buckland (1992, 64–65) believed that a library user anywhere with a computer should be able, from a single networked access point, to search the entire catalog, including bibliographies and reference works, and retrieve texts, images, audio, video, and numeric data. The terminology did not yet exist, but he was describing a federated search of an entirely digital collection.

These changes would lead to a greater emphasis on enabling self-service and "from a library-centered world view to one that that is user-centered" (Buckland 1992, 75). In many respects, these changes have been implemented and in a user-focused way, although not for those who need access to library-specific information or services in order to fulfill their digital or virtual needs. Electronic resources that can be accessed through Google, including Google properties like YouTube and Google Books, frequently meet Buckland's criteria—or come close enough to satisfy users. However, when users bring their open web–developed assumptions to the library for the first time, they are often surprised that so many electronic resources at libraries are inaccessible, poorly designed, or fail to interoperate. These limitations are the result of "conflicting interests between the stakeholders," such as vendors whose products are confined to "information silos," copyright- or license-restricted texts, and material that is not yet fully digitally accessible. While we appear to be transitioning to the Electronic Library, as Buckland foresaw, the impediments are rarely technological. For the most part, the technology was available within 10 years of the publication of *Redesigning Library Services* or soon thereafter. The obstacles to libraries offering a user-centered view of the world are now political and financial.

Situating Redesigning Library Services

In order to understand the context in which *Redesigning Library Services* was published, and to appreciate what Buckland knew about technology when he wrote it, it is helpful to remind ourselves about the state of computing and networking in 1992. Just over 20 million personal computers were sold that year, with IBM PCs and other PC-compatible computers accounting for about 85 percent of those sales, and Apple accounting for most of the rest, about 12 percent. A typical Apple computer at the time, such as the flagship Macintosh Classic II, had a 16 MHz CPU, came with 2 MB of RAM (expandable to 10 MB), had a 40 MB or 80 MB hard drive, a 9-inch black-and-white screen, and cost $1,900 (Apple Inc. 2012). In contrast, a base-model iMac purchased in August 2012 would include a processor that is more than 150 times faster, 2,000 times as much RAM, a hard drive that could store 12,500 times more data, a 21.5-inch color screen, and a cost of $700 less.

Clearly, most people who had computers in 1992 were using PCs, generally still with a DOS operating system, even though Windows 3.0 (released in 1990) and 3.1 (released in 1992) combined to sell 10 million copies during their first two years on the market (Microsoft 2012). In addition, IBM's OS/2 operating system was released in 1992 and attracted a strong initial following, selling about two million copies. It fleetingly appeared as though in the future OS/2 would compete with Windows and Apple's operating systems for a share of the desktop market (Reimer 2005). Instead, that third desktop operating system would eventually turn out to be Linux, which was announced in August 1991 by the 21-year-old Linus Torvalds, a computer science student in Helsinki. The first Linux distributions were released in 1992 and would soon become popular with academics, though Torvalds would not release what he considered a mature 1.0 version of the kernel until 1994 (Hasan 2005).

The Internet had existed for some time by 1992, though it was overwhelmingly text based until the University of Illinois NCSA Mosaic browser was released in November 1993, which was soon followed by the founding of Netscape as Mosaic Communications Corporation in April 1994. In 1992, the number of computers connected to the Internet passed the one million mark (Computer History Museum 2006).

Notably, Buckland refers to neither the Internet nor the World Wide Web by name in his *Manifesto*—it is useful to realize that the most significant technology of the next 10 or 20 years might have been emerging at that moment and may not have been considered particularly remarkable—though he does make several references to hypertext and to the implications of the newly released Z39.50 protocol and clearly understood the importance of computer networking in planning for the future of library services. He mentions, in the first page of the preface, that "[t]he on-line library catalog is probably the most sophisticated computer system of any type in routine, direct use by the general public" (Buckland 1992, ix), but he makes it clear throughout the book that he does not expect that situation to persist: "Paper and pen are being supplemented by desktop workstations capable of using a multiplicity of remote sources" (Buckland 1992, 75). In other words, what he anticipated, and welcomed, was the inexorable transition from the Paper Library, through the Automated Library, to the Electronic Library.

The Library of 2025 versus the 100-Year Library

It is important to acknowledge the difference between making predictions and plans that are useful for 10 or even 20 years, as Buckland's have proved to be, and those meant to encompass 100 years. What we need to do is calibrate our scale. As Buckland (1992, x) notes, "Bits and pieces of what is predicted here do not require a crystal ball as they are already happening"—meaning that in making predictions for the library of 2025, it makes sense to expand on what is already happening around us and not to invent wholly new ideas or anticipate seismic shifts. From our perspective looking forward 2025 seems far away. But once we have lived through the intervening years, they will seem to have happened quickly.

As a calibrating, complementary exercise, it is useful when making comparatively short-term predictions to spend a moment imagining what the library will look like in 100 years. Could we design that library today, just as La Fontaine and Otlet designed what we now know as contemporary information services almost a century before the technology to implement their design was available? If we could, would we want to start using it now?

These two questions are posed in Paul Graham's, "The Hundred-Year Language" (2003), an essay about designing a programming language. His answer to both questions was affirmative: we could start designing and using the 100-year language now, and we should, because people would prefer it to what we have today. I believe the answer to both questions, when applied to libraries, is affirmative as well. The key, as with any good design, is to match an understanding of what people would enjoy doing with the structural changes necessary to make it possible. The convergence of events that gave rise to modern libraries 150 years ago, and to the modern study of libraries 80 years ago, occurred in vastly different information environments from our own. But the societal values that libraries represent are likely to continue to be valuable for at least another 100 years: the ability to engage in and benefit from communal acquisition, organization, dissemination, preservation, and production of social goods and information, and to do so in person, yet also privately, confidentially, and with intellectual freedom intact.

The interaction of first principles with long time sequences is like the law of large numbers in probability theory: we cannot say with any degree of precision when libraries' first principles will counter the current irrationality of the e-book or scholarly publishing market. It could happen in 2020, 2030, 2040, or later still. But it seems safe to predict that, over the next 100 years, we will figure out immediate and convenient ways to get texts—regardless of their length, medium, or where they were originally published—to the people who want to make use of them.

In the interim between now and 100 years from now, we can also anticipate the next stage in modern library development. We understand the Paper Library and the Automated Library, and though it is not yet fully realized, we also understand what the Electronic Library will look like and how people will use it. What we are only now beginning to conceive of is the fourth stage in library development, the Participatory Library.

The Participatory Library

The first line of chapter 1 of *Redesigning Library Services* may, by 2025, be viewed as its most dated: "The central purpose of the library is to provide a service: access to information" (Buckland 1992, 1). Access is a means, not an end. The library of 2025 seems likely to have as its central purpose *enabling connection and creation*. Information in the form of texts and other media can be an ingredient in creation or connection. For instance, one of the primary reasons that many of us enjoy reading is because it connects us to the author, other readers, and the people who are represented by the characters and ideas in the text. We want to read books immediately after they are released, not only because they hold the promise of an entirely new experience, but also because other people are reading them, too.

We also enjoy creating our own stories and experiences around what we have read, whether extending the author's ideas, dressing as characters from the works, or using the works as a guide in more practical ways, such as learning an academic subject or vocational skill. Although information is frequently necessary in acts of connection and creation, it is often not sufficient. That means libraries need to provide more than just information and need to invest significant time, effort, and money into providing these complementary services—perhaps even more time and money, going forward, than we currently allocate to the activities associated with collecting and organizing information and with making it accessible.

In a recent article on the Participatory Library, authors Linh Cuong Nguyen, Helen Partridge, and Sylvia L. Edwards (2012) trace the genesis of the idea and provide a comprehensive overview of the library activities, services, and technologies that Participatory Library advocates support. The term itself was apparently coined in 2006 by R. David Lankes, Joanne Silverstein, and Scott Nicholson (2006) of the Syracuse University School of Information Studies in an issue brief prepared for the American Library Association's Office for Information Technology Policy. The ideas associated with the Participatory Library, especially the technologies associated with making libraries more participatory such as wikis, blogs, RSS, and social networks, were quickly promulgated, most notably by Michael E. Casey and Laura C Savastinuk (2007); Michael Stephens (2006, 2007); and Lankes, Silverstein, Nicholson, and Todd Marshall (2007). Somewhat more recent works extend the idea of the Participatory Library, including subsequent work by Lankes and by other thought leaders in library technology, such as John Blyberg and Meredith Farkas, who presented an ALA TechSource Webcast called "Building the Participatory Library" in 2010. Unfortunately, the excitement around the idea of the Participatory Library appears to have waned, along with excitement around the buzzwords with which it was initially associated, including Web 2.0, Library 2.0, and the aforementioned wikis, RSS, and other rapidly dated technologies.

The point of Library 2.0 was never about making library websites "cooler," however; it was about engaging library members, and potential members, in conversation. It was about finding out what they wanted, not just from their libraries but in their lives, and working with them to make sure they got it. And it was also about introducing them to new ideas and having them introduce us to new ideas. Ultimately, the Participatory Library is about a more equitable distribution of knowledge, experience, and opportunity, and about making sure people have as many choices available to them as possible. The ethos of the Participatory Library is the recognition that the more power resides outside the library, the better the library is performing. This is where our first principles are leading us. The point of preserving culture, the end purpose of the work libraries do to ensure privacy and intellectual freedom, is to maximize the power of individuals within the community we serve.

The Participatory Library can be identified by several characteristics, some of which have already begun to take hold. First, records and texts are available via unified search, made possible by more widely adopted standards, universal digitization, and licensing that serves those who wish to make use of texts. As this happens, currently ineffectual techniques like patron-driven acquisition will begin to flourish not just locally, but they will also benefit from network effects across consortia. Second, tasks associated with creation are seen by library members and the library as being at least as important as collection usage, and budgets and job descriptions are adjusted accordingly. This development is foreshadowed by the Maker Spaces movement described by Lauren Britton (2012) in *Library Journal*. Other libraries are pursuing similar efforts by developing hacker or coworking spaces, or have set up 3D printing labs, though many seem to view this as a standalone service rather than the cornerstone of a Maker Space. As creation becomes more central to their mission, libraries will also invest more time and money into helping would-be authors or makers create their work in ways that make it easy for would-be readers or users of their work to discover it.

A third characteristic of the Participatory Library is its emphasis on immersive virtual experiences, which is becoming more commonplace as displays, processing power, bandwidth speeds, and the tools needed to create objects with even richer stores of data proliferate. It is difficult to imagine a time in which these developments will not be made available in waves, with the richest and best-connected individuals having the earliest access, followed by those with fewer resources. In order to balance distribution, and in order to take advantage of efficiencies of scale, libraries will remain a place where people can share in the newest technologies and learn how they work. In addition, as more people have more access to virtual interactions, in-person experiences become more significant both from a financial standpoint and as authentic experience. As is currently the case in music and film, people value opportunities to share in experiences with others. Libraries remain at the nexus of this human impulse. Finally, the Participatory Library is embedded within its community, much like utilities are today. This is hinted at by Buffy Hamilton and David Shumaker, each of whom released a book in 2012 about embedded librarianship, and by Douglas County Libraries' community reference initiative (Galston et al. 2012).

Buckland refers to his predictions as assumptions and offers them as lists, several of which have been summarized above. I have an assumption/prediction as well: we will recognize the Participatory Library not by a renewed library presence, but by its seeming absence. At this writing, one of the most popular podcasts is a program about design, "99% Invisible," which celebrates the aspects of design we generally fail to notice. A popular current meme was initiated by designer Golden Krishna's (2012) blog post: "The best interface is no interface." As search becomes indistinguishable from the impulse to acquire, as the ability to access resources ceases to be a barrier in the process of creation, as technology becomes better able to imitate life (and the inimitable aspects of life, therefore, become even more highly valued), and as libraries develop the ability to make their services present where and when they are needed, what is and is not the library will be less readily defined, even as its utility as an institution grows exponentially.

References

Apple Inc. 2012. "Macintosh Classic II: Technical Specifications." Last modified April 19. https://support.apple.com/kb/SP204.

Britton, Lauren. 2012. "The Makings of Maker Spaces, Part 1: Space for Creation, Not Just Consumption." *The Digital Shift* (blog), October 1. www.thedigitalshift.com/2012/10/public-services/the-makings-of-maker-spaces-part-1-space-for-creation-not-just-consumption.

Buckland, Michael K. 1992. *Redesigning Library Services: A Manifesto*. Chicago: American Library Association. http://sunsite.berkeley.edu/Literature/Library/Redesigning/html.html.

Calhoun, Karen. 2006a. "The Catalog's Future." Presentation at ACRL Delaware Valley Chapter Fall Program, Bryn Mawr, Pennsylvania, November 3. http://acrldvc.org/index.php/download_file/view/52/91.

———. 2006b. *The Changing Nature of the Catalog and Its Integration with Other Discovery Tools*. Washington, DC: Library of Congress. www.loc.gov/catdir/calhoun-report-final.pdf.

Casey, Michael E., and Laura C. Savastinuk. 2007. *Library 2.0: A Guide to Participatory Library Service*. Medford, NJ: Information Today.

Computer History Museum. 2006. "Exhibits—Internet History—1990s." www.computerhistory.org/internet_history/internet_history_90s.html.

Galston, Colbe, Elizabeth Kelsen Huber, Katherine Johnson, and Amy Long. 2012. "Community Reference: Making Libraries Indispensable in a New Way." *American Libraries* (blog), June 13 (11:00 a.m.). http://americanlibrariesmagazine.org/features/06132012/community-reference-making-libraries-indispensable-new-way.

Graham, Paul. 2003. "The Hundred-Year Language." PaulGraham.com. http://paulgraham.com/hundred.html.

Hamilton, Buffy. 2012. *Embedded Librarianship: Tools and Practices*. Chicago: ALA TechSource.

Hasan, Ragib. 1999. "History of Linux." Department of Computer Science, University of Illinois at Urbana-Champaign. Last updated October 18, 2005. www.ragibhasan.com/linux.

Krishna, Golden. 2012. "The Best Interface Is No Interface." *Journal: A Blog about Design, Business and the World We Live In*, August 29. www.cooper.com/journal/2012/08/the-best-interface-is-no-interface.html.

Lankes, R. David, Joanne Silverstein, and Scott Nicholson. 2006. *Participatory Networks: The Library as Conversation*. Syracuse, NY: Information Institute of Syracuse, Syracuse University's School of Information Studies. www.ala.org/offices/sites/ala.org.offices/files/content/oitp/publications/booksstudies/Participatory%20Networ.pdf.

Lankes, R. David, Joanne Silverstein, Scott Nicholson, and Todd Marshall. 2007. "Participatory Networks: The Library as Conversation." *Information Research* 12, no. 4. http://informationr.net/ir/12-4/colis05.html.

"Michael Buckland." n.d. School of Information, University of California, Berkeley. http://people.ischool.berkeley.edu/~buckland/bio.html.

Microsoft. 2012. "A History of Windows: Highlights from the First 25 Years." Microsoft Windows. http://windows.microsoft.com/en-US/windows/history.

Nguyen, Linh Cuong, Helen Partridge, and Sylvia L. Edwards. 2012. "Towards an Understanding of the Participatory Library." *Library Hi Tech* 30, no. 2: 335–46.

Reimer, Jeremy. 2005. "Total Share: 30 Years of Personal Computer Market Share Figures." *Ars Technica* (blog), December 14 (11:00 a.m. CST). http://arstechnica.com/features/2005/12/total-share/7.

Shumaker, David. 2012. *The Embedded Librarian: Innovative Strategies for Taking Knowledge Where It's Needed*. Medford, NJ: Information Today.

Stephens, Michael. 2006. "Web 2.0 and Libraries: Best Practices for Social Software." *Library Technology Reports* (July/August). http://thehyperlinkedlibrary.org/libtechreport1.

———. 2007. "Web 2.0 and Libraries, Part 2: Trends and Technologies." *Library Technology Reports* (September/October). http://thehyperlinkedlibrary.org/libtechreport2.

Chapter 2

RADICAL TRUST

A User-Librarian Shared Model

Dave Harmeyer

Imagine a library in 2025 that over the years has yielded, progressively and resolutely, substantial control to the end user. Giving up this control is not simply asking patrons for opinions in the occasional focus group and encouraging them to contribute book reviews to the catalog. Rather, it is the complete abandonment of the classical gatekeeper-librarian model in favor of an equal, unrestricted, patron-librarian shared model. Sound scary? This seemingly egregious direction of future librarianship is nevertheless quite congruent with the natural evolution of Library 2.0, which in its heyday promised to "revitalize the way we serve and interact with our customers" (Casey and Savastinuk 2006, para. 2). A fundamental principle of Library 2.0 is something called "radical trust." Collin Douma coined the term in 2006 as a new marketing strategy that embraced the idea that engaging consumers in an open community could actually improve consumer trust and build a stronger brand. In libraries, radical trust is an outgrowth of librarian enthusiasm for the collaboration with and empowerment of patrons that became possible in online communities such as blogs or social networks. In libraries that employ social networking platforms such as Facebook and Twitter, end users have a measure of say, usually in the form of comments, in the workings of the library. This is the seed of radical trust in libraries, though its implications are much larger, much deeper, and surprisingly, not new.

The prominent twentieth-century library theorist Ranganathan appears to have addressed radical trust in his five laws of library science. Ranganathan's (1963) third law states, "Every book, its reader," which has been commonly interpreted to mean that librarians, with knowledge about the end user's interests and needs, select resources for the reader with little or no direct input. However, when Ranganathan's third law is interpreted through the framework of radical trust, an interpretation increasingly visible in today's libraries, the reader becomes a significant part of the selection process. This transition has taken place in recent years as libraries have begun to embrace greater patron-driven acquisitions, pay-per-view e-books, and increased emphasis on patron requests.

Visions of Radical Trust

Library 2.0, of course, borrowed its moniker from Web 2.0. Tim O'Reilly, who with Dale Dougherty and John Battelle created the term "Web 2.0," stated that one of the seven competences of Web 2.0 was "trusting users as codevelopers" (O'Reilly 2005). In digital environments, end users often take part knowingly in radical trust activities, but some users may take on a more distinctive, hidden role. In these environments, companies like Google unobtrusively collect and act upon data about users' information-seeking behavior, turning end users into unknowing codevelopers. For instance, Google uses details about users' aggregate searching behaviors to rank its search results. Furthermore, the company's privacy policy allows data from users' online behavior to be leveraged to determine the display of individualized ads during searches (Google 2012). In a similar vein, O'Reilly (2005, under "End of Software Release Cycle") recalls, "A web developer at a major online service remarked: 'We put up two or three new features on some part of the site every day, and if users don't adopt them, we take them down. If they like them, we roll them out to the entire site.'" Quietly turning website users into trusted codevelopers not only improves a system without the user's laborious and possibly reluctant involvement but also affects future positive engagement and loyalty between the users and the system.

Another classic case of radical trust in action is Wikipedia, a web service built on the audacious idea that it could be possible for the online community to collaboratively write an encyclopedia without editorial oversight. Interestingly, the framework for Wikipedia comes from Eric Raymond's principle, based on observations of programmers working with open source code, that "with enough eyeballs, all bugs are shallow" (Merrill 2012). In other words, given enough codevelopers in a system, most—if not all—mistakes will be seen and fixed. According to this theory, the online community as a whole will self-regulate and correct each other's errors.

A final model of radical trust in Web 2.0 is tagging, the almost ubiquitous online ability to label things with terms decided exclusively by the user, which can be found in popular applications like del.icio.us and Flickr. Tagging is an open and fluid form of information organization, in contrast to the closed categories found in the controlled vocabulary of library subject headings. In 2008, the Library of Congress released 4,600 photographs on Flickr, and the site's membership populated them with tens of thousands of tags and thousands of comments that made these images suddenly visible and discoverable for a dramatically wider audience than ever before (Springer et al. 2008). This type of deep integration of librarian and user as codevelopers in information organization has yet to be fully expressed in Library 2.0. Still, there have been a few flag-wavers advocating greater radical trust for the profession of librarianship.

Advocates of Radical Trust for Libraries

On March 19, 2006, librarian Darlene Fichter posted on Flickr an image of Einstein writing on a chalkboard the formula "Library 2.0 = (books 'n stuff + people + radical trust) × participation" as a way to advance the principle of radical trust (Fichter 2006). So what does this formula mean? Fichter elaborates in an April 2, 2006, blog posting:

> Libraries have always been about books 'n stuff and people. The notion of radical trust and applying this to online library activities introduces a new dimension to the work that we've been doing in libraries. . . . We can only build emergent systems if we have radical trust. . . . We don't have a million customers/users/patrons . . . we have a million participants and co-creators. Radical trust is about trusting the community. (Fichter 2006)

Fichter believes in the sustainability of the library, but only if end users participate in the cocreation of the new library.

Other early flag-wavers for radical trust are Lankes, Silverstein, and Nicholson (2007), although they refer instead to the "participatory library." The participatory library is "the idea that a participating library as a truly integrated library system must allow users to take part in core functions of the library like the catalogue system" (Nguyen, Partridge, and Edwards 2012, 335). The idea of participatory librarianship is framed as an ongoing conversation between large numbers of users and facilitator-librarians. Research has shown that

> . . . under the right circumstances, groups are remarkably intelligent, and are often smarter than the smartest people in them. Groups do not need to be dominated by exceptionally intelligent people in order to be smart. Even if most of the people within a group are not especially

well-informed or rational, it can still reach a collectively wise decision. (Surowiecki 2004, xiii)

Participatory librarianship makes claims on at least five library areas: reference, cataloging, collection development, strategic planning, and publicity. In the area of reference, both librarians and end users answer questions and respond to each other on public websites and blogs like Ask.com and Allexperts.com. Another application of participatory librarianship is folksonomy, a system of classification with no set controlled vocabulary where terms (or tags) are determined solely by end users. The collective number of tags creates the classification for an item. The participatory library is on a larger scale, outside the physical and virtual walls of the conventional library.

Users enter participatory librarianship as collection development advisors when they suggest resources to acquire via a library's website or leave a review on a book, media item, or journal article with recommendations through a library's social media presence. End users function as library administrators by critiquing publicly posted drafts of strategic plans and library policies. Patrons with blogs, wikis, and social media accounts can easily publicize a library's website, programs, and online resources or even link to the library from their own reviews of items held by the library. Users can also recommend print or online items to be added to a library's research guides for topical interest and research. Radical trust, or participatory librarianship, has been making influential inroads into the traditional views of the librarian community where "temple guardians" were once overseers of sacred resources.

There are several elephant-in-the-room reasons why library leaders should be serious about radical trust. Radical trust addresses some of the greatest threats to library sustainability, including the following:

- Disintermediation
- Changes in end users' information-seeking behavior
- Changes in user demographics
- Perception that the library is becoming marginalized in the accreditation process
- Severe budget challenges
- Significant financial increases in online resources
- The growing popularity of mobile devices such as smartphones and tablets

Based on these and other potentially threatening trends, there is very likely radical change ahead for the profession. However, current thinking about the future of the library appears to be blind to these threats. With these obser-vations in mind, the remainder of this chapter proposes two scenarios: the first describes what a library would look like in the year 2025 without radi-cal trust, and the second describes what a library would look like in the year 2025 with radical trust.*

Scenario One: The Library 2025 without Radical Trust, or Resistance Is Futile

Back in 2015, the Springfield Public Library director implemented the begin-nings of the library's next five-year strategic plan. The plan's focus on cooper-ating with four other public libraries in the ownership of shared collections of lesser-used print materials would make it possible for the library to allocate more funding to technology and comfortable seating. A suitable facility was chosen as the off-site location to store the shared print collection. A local cou-rier service had been arranged with a promised turnaround time of less than 48 hours. Then the libraries involved were suddenly faced with severe finan-cial cuts and the plan was canceled. At about this time, city council members were contacted by a corporation representative with a proposal for a complete takeover of the financially weakened public library and a promise to turn it around to both be more efficient and produce a better return on investment. The deal was done in less than six months, and the new owners of Springfield Public Library put their business plan into action.

The Springfield Public Library takeover involved a number of immediate changes. First, all personnel were put on notice to begin looking for other em-ployment since any contracts were considered void. Union employees, though few in number, were dealt with on a case-by-case basis and were allowed to be interviewed for new positions immediately. Any former employee could also apply for new positions, but many did not. In order to maintain the li-brary's minimum daily functions, a team of corporate library associates re-placed all personnel during the transition and the library's doors remained open to the public.

The personnel protocols for newly hired library staff were designed for efficiency. The business model required any new hire, with no regard to ex-perience or education, to go through five days of library associate training. A similar training would be required every six months until a certain level of

* Scenario two is adapted from the author's 2010 article "Blending the Reference In-terview and Information Literacy; Reference Interviews: A Series of Personal Refer-ence Stories," *The Reference Librarian* 51, no. 4: 358–62.

proficiency was met, at which time the associate would be required to attend such training only once a year. Training included understanding and embracing the new business model involving Six Sigma management strategies with an emphasis on cutting costs. Preparation also included deep team-building exercises, conflict management, customer service paradigms, and the development of step-by-step processes for certain predetermined projects that had clear objectives and data-driven, quantifiable outcomes. Several assessment efforts had been automated, including circulation, reference inquiries, head counts, and patron surveys, making data gathering a much less time-intensive task. A Master of Library and Information Science (MLIS) degree from an accredited American Library Association program was a nonnegotiable requirement for some positions. But everyone, regardless of former rank, training, or experience, was referred to as a library associate except the "lead associate," who acted as a director.

After a year of training, hiring new positions, and stabilizing routines, a different financial model was put in place. All patrons would need to become library members to check out materials by paying an annual fee based on their individual or joint tax bracket. The justification was easy: deep cuts in library revenue from government sources necessitated a pay-as-you-go solution. In order to honor the library's long-standing commitment to equal access to information for all, a perpetual charitable funding campaign called the Carnegie Vision was established to provide generous scholarships for those unable to pay the membership fee.

At the company's main office, a charge went out to the creative design department to implement the most captivating marketing campaign in library history for the Carnegie Vision. Several professionally developed video ads were created and broadcast on the library's double-sided, 50-inch, high-definition retina screens. The display could be devoted to one large video image, such as the Carnegie Vision campaign ads interspersed with documentaries of Carnegie's life. The screen's technology, though, also allowed for a seamless segue into four equally sized displays. One of the four quadrants would run the Carnegie Vision, a second and third quadrant contained two live feeds—one from a popular national news syndication and the second a local/national sports broadcast (which was selected based on feedback from company-run surveys of local memberships)—and the final quadrant ran information literacy instruction videos about the library's web-based applications. All four screens had real-time closed-captioning and optional ear buds (checked out from the main desk) that allowed users to hear any of the four channels in a number of different languages, including the top three represented by library membership and the area's demographics. The same visual publicity and information literacy were streamed on the library's website and adapted to carefully scripted social networking postings. As an incentive to increase membership and capitalize on the ad campaign, one of the screens was placed in a high traffic area elsewhere in the city.

In addition to a different funding model of membership fees and charitable donations, most of the former in-house tasks were outsourced for better efficiency and cost-saving strategies. This included collection development, acquisitions, and cataloging. All three areas were transferred to three separate but highly collaborative subdivisions of the company housed at the corporate main office. Collection development was directly tied to the demographics surrounding Springfield Library. Through highly integrated cable and dish networks, public surveys were regularly filled out by area residents on personal mobile devices, which asked about preferences for a number of consumer products as well as library resources. Highly tailored lucrative incentives for filling out the surveys ensured reliable, consistent data for the corporate office.

Appropriate collection requests were almost instantly fulfilled. These orders were automatically sent to the acquisitions division, where they were added to a predetermined list of library print and e-book orders that included titles found on weekly fiction, nonfiction, trade, and mass-market bestseller lists. Orders for digital formats were filled in real time. All orders, of course, were at a discounted bulk price. Finally, the cataloging division added items to the local catalog where records were enhanced with local identifying tags and value-added content like video book trailers, holographic 3D book covers, author interviews, first and last pages, and reviews by both expert and amateur reviewers. Company experts cataloged local historical artifacts, documents, and archival special collections for the immediate area surrounding the library.

The investment finally turned a profit for the company after nine years of training, deep change, and exceptional customer service. All library associates received an additional 2 percent in their retirement accounts and a $500 cash bonus. The financial future of Springfield Library now appears to be in the black, and that's good news for members, library associates, the company, and the sustainability of corporate-run libraries. Since those very difficult days 10 years ago, Springfield Public Library is now one of about a quarter of the nation's public libraries owned and operated by a corporation. A few of the companies are subsidiaries of publishing giants, some members of Fortune 500, and certainly most are invested in providing access to digital information. Digital access companies that own libraries provide deep discounts for their so-called library franchises, discounts that are not equally offered to publicly supported libraries. As a result, a group of deans and directors from other public and academic libraries have filed a class action lawsuit against three of these library-owning publishing companies, with the charges being conflict of interest and price-fixing. The likely result of the case is as yet unclear.

Scenario Two: The Library 2025 with Radical Trust, or the Athenaeum

In early spring of 2015, Brett University's dean of the library began a deliberate plan to incorporate radical trust into her organization using Future Search, a consecutive three-day event at which a large number of stakeholders come to make consensus-driven future plans on a particular issue (Weisboard and Janoff 2010). The first Future Search topic was this: "Describe the library of the future that would meet your expectations and keep you coming back." The event planners invited over 60 participants from diverse stakeholder groups, such as students, faculty, administrators, and board members. This weekend and subsequent Future Search events profoundly changed how Brett's library personnel, campus administrators, and faculty viewed library users. It also heightened an appreciation of radical trust and ways in which librarians and users could codevelop a library of the future. The seeds planted at that first event altered the original building plans and expanded the purposes of Brett's new library building, which was completed in 2022.

It's been 10 years since that first Future Search and three since the completion of the new facility. A visitor's tour of the busy, thriving space offers some evidence of a consistent radical trust focus. Upon entering the expansive lobby, on the right is suspended a 100-inch plasma retina touch screen displaying, among other innovations, a digital message board, live-captioned news feed, and a large image of the three-story building. By lightly touching any one of dozens of spots on the screen, a window opens revealing text and video explaining that area of the structure. An approachable circular central information desk staffed by student assistants and professional librarians is found surrounded by comfortable chairs, where one can receive tablet or mobile device assistance, information literacy instruction, research consulting, and a calendar of events, and request and retrieve books and resources.

It was the building's name, however, that intrigued visitors the most: it was called the Athenaeum. Touching the name "Athenaeum" on the digital screen begins a video whose narrator is not a polished professional speaker nor a librarian, but an adult student in one of Brett's degree programs. She explains that the name was chosen because of the extreme diversity within the new structure, and she mentions that the library is one of many campus units inhabiting the space. We learn that any project can be started and completed in the 24/7/365-day facility, as students can make use of a series of expert areas such as a writing center, technology support desks, a document copying and mobile device printing room, a graphic arts studio, and a publishing corner.

More innovations highlighted on the tour reflect the impact of the radical trust model of user-librarian collaborative decision making. Because Future Search participants expressed a deep interest in accessing print books, the Athenaeum's basement contains a million-volume capacity automated retrieval system, designed as a closed stacks area, with an additional area of conventional open shelving for 5,000 of the most current and in-demand volumes. At the information desk users can request a print book from the basement and have it retrieved for them in less than 10 minutes. Virtual students have the option of requesting books electronically via an innovative system that digitizes a 200-page book in 30 minutes, gains copyright clearance, and sends the file anywhere in the world. This system came about as an idea championed during a recent Future Search event by a doctoral faculty member whose students are on campus only four weeks out of the year.

At the request of many Future Search participants, a food court was included on the main floor with no restrictions except in two quiet study spaces. During the initial Future Search weekend, three students, all in the physical education program, promoted the idea of including workout machines in the library, thinking they would draw users who might not feel comfortable coming to a conventional space. In response, the Athenaeum includes five treadmills and five exercise bikes on the second floor balcony. Additionally, because Brett U's primary student population was older adult learners, a number of parent student participants in Future Search expressed a need for reliable, affordable childcare during classes and extended research time. A childcare center is located on the main floor in a soundproof area with access to inside and outside age-appropriate playgrounds. Adult students can easily drop off children up to 13 years old at the subsidized facility, which is run by faculty and students in the human development section of the P–12 educational program.

To strengthen, deepen, and perpetuate the radical trust experience, the dean of the library inaugurated more Future Search events covering various topics, including some sacred cows of librarianship: information literacy, cataloging, and copyright. The conversations that took place in these sessions shaped the direction of the Athenaeum, increasing the participation of users in the day-to-day operations of the library, creating new partnerships that embedded librarians across campus, and spurring everyone to engage in library issues.

Conclusion

In this chapter, two scenarios were presented, the first without the equal codeveloper focus necessary for radical trust to be realized and the second taking the opposite approach. Both scenarios addressed a number of current challenges faced by the library community, but in very different ways. The real library of 2025 will likely include elements of both scenarios. With this in mind, it may be useful to conclude with some reflection on the two scenarios in light of how they address the challenges mentioned earlier.

Scenario One is the more disturbing of the two for today's librarians. Four challenges addressed by the first scenario are changes in end users' information-seeking behavior, changes in user demographics, severe budget challenges, and significant financial increases in online resources. The business model in Scenario One demands accurate data through extensive, ongoing surveys to quickly meet and clearly understand customers' needs, wants, and behaviors, including information seeking. It is an efficient system that would notice changes in user demographics and adjust to language, age, cultural background, or any other demographic for tailor-made resources and services.

Significant cost increases to online resources is lethal to library budgets. In the first scenario there is an added dynamic as the distributor of online content becomes the library's owner or close partner. If the financial budgets are kept at the corporate level, funding decisions are negotiated on a large discount to keep online resource costs unusually low. Finally, the corporate story deals with severe budget challenges by a business plan that eventually pays off, a profit is maintained and employees are rewarded. On the other hand, these corporate-owned libraries threaten the well-being of other libraries around the nation, as evidenced by the class action lawsuit filed by those libraries.

In Scenario One it could be argued that there are at least two radical trust-type interactions between corporate decision makers and users or potential users—namely, company-run surveys of local members and company-run surveys filled out by residents near to the library. However, in Scenario One both types of surveys have been used in the corporate-run library setting for many years without the special collaborative rigor needed between corporate decision makers and library users to satisfy a radical trust model. These two types of surveys focus on gathering data about resources and services that the corporation can easily fulfill within its business model and not the significant changes users would demand that would put them at the level of true library codevelopers. In this scenario users are seen as relatively unempowered consumers and certainly not radical trust codevelopers.

Scenario Two is the more hopeful of the two stories. Three problems from the introduction that are addressed in Scenario Two are disintermediation, a perception that the library is becoming marginalized in the accreditation process, and the growing popularity of mobile devices like smartphones and tablets. The scenario addresses disintermediation by including end users in the mediation process. Librarians are persuaded to meet students on their own turf (their dorms), to focus on empowering student users as copresenters in library instruction and reference desk interviews and to run a student peer-to-peer service that teaches information literacy skills.

Although Scenario Two represents only one academic library, administrators and board members who were affected by radical trust and participated in a Future Search were certainly more informed about the library's conversations with end users as well as the importance the library plays in the mission of the university. The library becomes more likely to be a noted player in national and state accreditation processes. If nothing else, this scenario reflects an academic library design that was integrated with technology, adding state-of-the-art devices and systems such as a plasma retina touch screen at the entrance and an automated retrieval system downstairs for print materials, both included in the design because of direct input from users. Student assistants and librarians at the circular information desk can assist with any mobile devices like smartphones and tablets or any other up-and-coming device used by students and faculty for educational purposes.

In the end, it is not clear how radical trust might play a part in the sustainability of librarianship. The scenarios presented in this chapter provide two possible visions for that future from opposite ends of the spectrum. Radical trust, though never fully realized in Library 2.0, could provide lasting solutions to address many of the challenges faced by librarianship today. Reaching out to stakeholders and including them in the decision-making process is the only way to ensure that libraries evolve in a direction that will continue to serve their needs. Google and other corporate entities realized this years ago and have been both incorporating user feedback into their product development and providing platforms for open communities of consumers. Only the years will tell if radical trust, with all its possibilities, will become the sine qua non of the library of 2025 and beyond.

References

Casey, Michael E., and Laura C. Savastinuk. 2006. "Library 2.0." *Library Journal* 131 (September 1): 40–2.

Douma, Collin. 2006. "Radical Trust." *Marketing Magazine* 111, no. 28: 16.

Fichter, Darlene. 2006. "Web 2.0, Library 2.0 and Radical Trust: A First Take." *Blog on the Side*. April 2. http://library.usask.ca/~fichter/blog_on_the_side/2006/04/web-2.html.

Google. 2012. "Privacy Policy." *Google Policies and Principles*. www.google.com/intl/en/policies/privacy.

Lankes, R. David, Joanne Silverstein, and Scott Nicholson. 2007. "Participatory Networks: The Library as Conversation." *Information Technology and Libraries* 26, no. 4: 17–33.

Merrill, Scott. 2012. "With Many Eyeballs, All Bugs Are Shallow." *TechCrunch* (blog), Thursday, February 23. http://techcrunch.com/2012/02/23/with-many-eyeballs-all-bugs-are-shallow.

Nguyen, Linh Cuong, Helen Partridge, and Sylvia L. Edwards. 2012. "Towards an Understanding of the Participatory Library." *Library Hi Tech* 30, no. 2: 335–46.

O'Reilly, Tim. 2005. "What Is Web 2.0: Design Patterns and Business Models for the Next Generation of Software." *O'Reilly Media, Inc.* http://oreilly.com/web2/archive/what-is-web-20.html.

Ranganathan, S. R. 1963. *The Five Laws of Library Science*. Bombay: Asia Publishing House.

Springer, Michelle, Beth Dulabahn, Phil Michel, Barbara Natanson, David Reser, David Woodward, and Helena Zinkham. 2008. *For the Common Good: The Library of Congress Flickr Pilot Project*. www.loc.gov/rr/print/flickr_report_final.pdf.

Surowiecki, James. 2004. *The Wisdom of Crowds: Why the Many Are Smarter Than the Few and How Collective Wisdom Shapes Business, Economies, Societies, and Nations*. New York: Doubleday.

Weisbord, Marvin, with Sandra Janoff. *Improving Performance in the Workplace. Volume 2: Selecting and Implementing Performance Interventions,* chap. 4, eds. Ryan Watkins and Doug Leigh. San Francisco: Pfeiffer/John Wiley, 2010.

Part 2

Reimagining Spaces

Chapter 3

MEANINGFUL SPACE
IN A DIGITAL AGE

Ben Malczewski

The imagination loses vitality as it ceases to adhere to what is real.

—*Wallace Stevens* (1965)

The presage arrived one night while I was watching TV in my family room in the form of a Microsoft commercial featuring a cool-by-committee couple praising the glories of the "almighty Cloud." My imagination gathered that the "C" should be capitalized, owing to the exultant background choral praise when the words were annunciated. The couple had never asked to be stuck in an airport with a flight delay, and now on top of that they were without personalized media entertainment. Being so close to hell, one questioned if an ethereal glance would even be worth it. Well, they needn't look *all the way* to heaven for answers—halfway would do. In an epiphany the husband remembers the Cloud, by which they can stream to their Windows-ready devices any of the content they would enjoy at home. "Yay Cloud!" Remembering that only the drought-stricken saw clouds as anything but portentous and feeling immediately threatened, I looked first at my coolly rendered vinyl record covers, my special edition DVDs, photographs, and books, and then to the furniture that was designed to hold and display their analog shapes. I felt their surface identities as unique-to-medium creative expressions and projections of my own memory and identity fade to nostalgia and sepia-tone before my eyes, devalued and devoid under this catch-all umbrella: "content."

This predicament was difficult for a pop-culture geek who also happened to be a librarian. In the case of DVDs, the former felt his love for box art, special edition sets, extras, voice-over commentaries, alternative endings, deleted scenes, outtakes, foreign versions, uncorrected errors, and signed editions threatened, while the latter saw the dismantling of these passionately

archived document assemblages—many of them painstakingly researched anthropological time capsules in their own right (by Criterion, Kino, etc.)—as
a deconstruction, *not* in a manner revealing essence but rather devolution-
ary. This should not be misread as an instanced lament for "things past" or
some subjective dirge for media I've falsely personified, or a feeling akin to
that fateful awkwardness when new puppy is brought home to meet old dog.
I consider myself a tech-centric librarian, and having presented and written
extensively on the evolution of AV and emerging technologies, I should be
unshaken in this regard. I am not against cloud computing, which in itself is
nothing new. But the mainstreaming of it was new, and in this sense it had
never hit home for me before.

As a consequence of this revelation I began to consider the practical and
emotional relationships we have with all of our "stuff" and how its acquisition and ownership have shaped and organized our physical world. The interior purposing of our living and working places, particularly in libraries,
has been designed for and around analog technology. So how does a shift to
a completely digitized content environment actualize itself physically? How
will our personal and public spaces look as a result? A great deal of space in
my home is dedicated to books, music, and movies, and indeed they have become part of the aesthetic and character of my style. What now if they were
suddenly deleted? Reconceptualizing our notion of content means redefining
the functionalism of our physical settings and, in effect, embracing the digitization of our homes, lives, and libraries.

When Did My "Stuff" Become Content?

We don't typically think of our possessions as content. In fact, we wouldn't
even think to refer to them so coldly as "possessions"—rather simply calling
them by name—and the word is hardly a colloquial synonym for books, films,
or music. The word "content" seems reserved for fluorescently lit back-end
technical discussion. It feels impersonal and lacks character and personality,
and thus associability. It feels like bar code data representation and inasmuch
as we are not ourselves bar code readers, we cannot extract meaning from it,
nor make a connection. Content in this definitive state doesn't give us anything to emotionally connect with, nor does it identify itself or speak to us or
in any way. It is the encryption of substance.

The questions "What sort of content do you like?" or "Did you see the latest comically toned nonfictional content based on the experiences of domestic
cats on YouTube?" would evoke little more than a disturbed, confused look. It
just doesn't seem human, and there is a good reason for this. We didn't happen

upon these forms of "content" by accident. We thought about them, studied them, got to know their voices, learned how they did what they did and why they were different, and might have even been pleasingly perplexed by them. To a degree, we saw or heard ourselves in them, or discovered an approach that directly or indirectly was congruent with our interests, fascinations, or worldview. Or maybe we just *wanted* to see ourselves in them or aspired to *be* them. And so we acquired them and brought them to our homes, where they became intimates; we connected and identified with them and they, in turn, became extensions of ourselves and symbolic reflections of who we are.

Whether the same emotional connection can be derived from electronic content is difficult to say. The removal of the tangible element removes a level in which we connect with the work, reasonably suggesting in the process a devaluing of the product itself if we cannot possess and thus connect with it in the same way. Inwardly, the information or idea can still be conveyed, but the physical relationship between self and stuff disappears. Physically displayed content brings multiple meaningful dimensions and extrapolations to our spaces, and its removal would no doubt make the space feel barren, as if to void the space of life itself. One e-reader on the proverbial shelf doesn't have the representative effect of even a single physical book with its unique cover design (color palette, font, etc.). What is to happen when the bookshelf is emptied, and then what becomes the point of the bookshelf? How will anyone know that you have read *The Great Gatsby* or think that you actually read *Ulysses*?

This depiction of depersonalized space is rooted in a cinematic sci-fi vision of the future—sometimes sterile, sometimes septic, but frequently soulless and humorless. Those characterless "living" rooms designed solely for the procedural now seem potential harbingers, suggesting that our future relationship with our surroundings might feel as disconnected as an actor cast against a green screen. If content is the encryption of substance, it also is an idea in search of a container, as it is rendered incommunicable and ineffective without a vehicle. Though oversimplified, it is often displaced that e-readers, tablets, computers, or even books themselves in general are empty vessels only as "good" or as useful as the content (in its many manifestations) they provide. Though we're easily distracted by the container, for technology in its exoticism has always been "sexy," it has always been about the content (whether file or software). An e-reader has little purpose without an e-book, just as much as a book with blank pages, while priceless as a metaphor, says nothing itself. The same can be said of rooms, buildings, and by extension libraries, as they are at least in literal terms (and however one-dimensionally) defined by the content they house.

The Projection of Self through Our Spaces

We have a neurologically rooted tribal relationship with our physical world. As social animals, human beings need some form of community: whether cave, cabin, condo, or club, we have gathered for protection and food and have formed tribes and exhibited tribal behavior. As civilization has advanced, our tribes have become more numerous and specific, developing into institutions, communities, and countries. With the proliferation of Internet-based social networking channels like Facebook and Twitter, we have expanded from face-to-face communication to create an exponentially more expansive and powerful paradigm of tribalism online. Networking catalysts can revolve around nearly anything imaginable, including sports teams, food, bands, movies, styles, clothing, hatreds, and loves.

Regardless of the increased capacity for communicative reach and the virtual relocation of our meeting "places," the predominant characteristic of tribes throughout time has remained the same: fulfilling the need to communicate. And actually, when you consider the terminology, nomenclature, and conceptualization of the virtual "architecture," hardly anything has changed. We design and decorate both our physical and virtual worlds the same way, carefully revealing the story of ourselves authored by ourselves as we would like it to be told. Our spaces become projections of ourselves, reflecting how we want to be seen and what we want others to think of us, but mostly how we want to see ourselves. It is no coincidence that these two worlds conceptually resemble each other, because in the end they must fulfill the same function as an outward and inward projection of self.

In this sense, the physical presentation of our books, DVDs, photos, paintings, and albums is no different than their JPEG or hyperlinked doppelgängers. They become avatars that reveal our identities to the outside world, telling others what bands we listen to, what our favorite movies are, what books we've read, and perhaps of equal importance, what bands we want others to *think* we like, what movies we want to be associated with, and what books we think will make us seem more erudite. And, just as in "real" life, the primary audience for our projection is actually ourselves. In an abstract way, we think and suppose what someone else might be thinking of us based on what we feel these objects symbolize or represent. A book on a shelf is straightforwardly a source of information or knowledge, but it may also represent both inwardly and outwardly an achievement or a demonstration of worldliness or sophistication. This demonstrates our self-conscious awareness of our subconscious, and it speaks to the emotional relationship we have with our physical spaces and the vital role objects play in the creation of identity for ourselves and others.

But what of this "line" that is crossed or connection that is made when our content becomes a mirror, and then a projection, of self? It is the moment when the objective becomes subjective. The effectual crux of when an outward (objective) object was internalized (subjective) was a primary focus of the imagism school of poetry established by Ezra Pound, T. E. Hulme, and F. S. Flint. Pound (1916) referred to it as when "[a] thing outward and objective transforms itself, or darts into a thing inward and subjective" (103), and described the moment of transformation as presenting "an intellectual and emotional complex in an instant of time . . . which gives that sudden sense of liberation . . . which we experience in the presence of great works of art" (99). James Joyce described the connective spark as an epiphany. We may not take such a powerful hyperbolic leap every time we read or watch a film, but every object (not just content) that inhabits our world was hand-selected by us because of how well we understand it (and its role or function), how it complements our experience and worldview, and also because of how well it communicates with us. When we physically hold a movie or a book, an emotional connection is made with the work. We associate with it and display this relationship; we project it to others and in turn see ourselves in it. Characterizing our personal spaces and adorning our public ones with physical objects not only decorates our rooms but lets others know where we've been, who we like, what we've read, what we listen to, and what our influences are.

Just as we internalize the artistic expression and often create our own subtextual relationship and sense memories around it (where we first saw it, who we were with, what we ate, what the weather was like, etc.), this continues with the physical product. Its presence on our shelf is akin to a photo album or diary. This is the self as personal historian, and objects as such become vital pillars in creating a sense of self through our past. Our memories of our past largely define our *selves*: who we believe we are. "People with amnesia who cannot remember their pasts say that they do not know who they are, that they have lost their 'selves'" (Schacter 1996). Content in this sense is unsociable encryption, as it communicates nothing. By personalizing space, we stimulate memory and reinforce a sense of who we are. Zeisel writes, "We can call environmental cues that have these effects *environmental personalization memory cues* (2006, 357). For those with healthy brains, small environmental cues such as carrying a picture of family members can achieve this memory stimulation." Our objects are autobiographical memory anchors of our chronology.

Creating Meaningful Spaces

It can seem somewhat thankless, but something is deemed successfully designed when we don't think about it while using it. A goal in the design of anything, whether tool, building, room, or floor plan, is to usher any work involved in its use or navigation to a lower level of consciousness, creating a natural and easy thoughtlessness. We feel, for example, most comfortable writing with a pen when we are not thinking about holding our grip on the pen. Good design is innovative (it should deliver a service more efficiently or lead more enjoyably to a destination) and aesthetic (it is pleasing to the eye or thematically aligned to function), and makes a product or service intuitively understandable. It is honest, unobtrusive, lasting, and consistent in every detail. It is environmentally friendly and feels as little "designed" as possible. In terms of floor plans, we are only conscious of our "wayfinding" in the library when we can't find something or when the path set forth is unclear (we cannot decipher public from staff space, signage is poor, etc.). There is a degree of acceptable "wandering" that we will put up with before we react by seeking help, getting frustrated, or just leaving.

When dealing with change or loss, as in the case of books or other format delivery methods, it is important to remember that while these are contributory parts of an experience, they are not *the* experience. We can repurpose space while still keeping our identity. As content and processes go virtual, our biggest obstacle to overcome as librarians in such conceptual transitions will often be our own reluctance and opposition to change. It's hard not to feel the ghosts of our lost materials. However, empty space left in their absence should not be kept as a vacant memorial to bygone formats, but rather replaced by something else or something better. In fact, all space will have to be reconsidered as flow, as focal points and destinations change. This is the equivalent of taking the TV out of the "TV room." The purposeful directives of the room will need to be redefined.

Physical print collections once easily consumed half of most libraries' physical space, yet in many cases, most of the collection has never circulated (e.g., see Cornell University Library 2010). Removing or relocating little-used materials frees library spaces for study, collaboration, meetings, and instruction. With an electronically accessible collection, spaces to engage will themselves become destinations. Rooms become open slates, and while we as librarians may cast a shadow of a room's former identity on the redesigned room, a person first experiencing the space will know nothing of its past. In many ways the removal of formats, which may be bulky or cost more in real estate than they generate in contributory value, can be liberating.

Narrative Design

When attempting to assess design and space relations by examining how and why we use spaces in the manner we do, the approaches commonly used are patron interviews, focus groups (with designers, architects, librarians, and patrons), and observation. We ask, "How do we behave in certain contexts?" and "What are perceived to be the distance limits and extents of personal space?" In attempting to create meaningful spaces in libraries, I began looking at how space was "used" and how we behaved in it. Applying the anthropological practice of proxemics, or the study of the cultural use of space, can help us understand how library patrons use (and expect to use) library spaces. Variables such as the distance between where people sit (when seating isn't ordered, as on a subway train), the degree of eye contact, the shoulder axis (open or closed) of two people, the degree of touching (or nontouching), and vocal volume observed unobtrusively can help us gain an idea of where and how rooms might be arranged. How people order nonfixed space (where they consistently move chairs or tables or if they substitute one style of chair for another) is a large component of designing *after* design as well and shows that it is a perpetual process.

In seeking to create intimate and meaningful public spaces, it dawned on me in the writing of this chapter that perhaps the most unbiased and "pure" observation subject was right in front of my eyes. I began observing how my one-year-old daughter engaged a book or handheld video as an uncontaminated indication of how people interact with content in personal spaces. As we get older it becomes more difficult to pinpoint the habitual roots, as our hows and whys become buried under much empirical and repressive clutter and behind so many centric lenses. In watching my relatively experience-free daughter I noticed that her enjoyment of the process had less to do with the content than it did with her *occasioning* of it. Similar to a director setting her mise-en-scène or a chef arranging his mise en place, the reading of a book or watching of a video was simply a component ingredient of a larger collective experience. What was most important was the pillow or chair on which to sit, the blanket, the water bottle, and the stuffed animal. She was staging factors into place that added up to the sum of her desired experience. She was not just constructing a scene but defining a space.

Her *occasioning* of space is similar to how patrons use the library. The content, though a necessary component of the experience, is more symbolic (the subject may change from day to day just like the delivering vessel), and in this flexibility it becomes less of a conditional onus than the atmosphere in which they will behold and learn it. So long as the information is present and pertinent to study, the environmental conditions set to facilitate the process rise to primary importance. If content is a constituent but not necessarily the most important part of the experience, the question becomes, "How can we develop a library space that people can feel comfortable enough to learn in?" Considering the notion of the library as experience (and locating an emotional definition of what a library means), the effort in manufacturing such an experience for patrons hinges on the extent to which we can develop a common subjective language. What are the communal equivalents of my daughter's pillow, blanket, bottle, and stuffed animal?

Our awareness of place is critical to the definition of memory, and our physical environment is therefore essential to memory constitution. In order to be experienced as a memory, the information we retrieve must be recollected in the context of a particular time and place and with reference to oneself as a participant in the episode, often in a multisensory capacity. In other words, in order for an event or action to have meaning in our lives, we have to play an active role in the narrative. Architecture and design are communicative arts that tell a story, but the paradox of ideological design is that we cannot speak with certainty about what the human individual actually experiences. We can have an interpretation, or maybe even share the dominant or a popular one, but subjective processing eliminates the possibility for an objective and ultimate universal truth. As a result, even if we agree on certain aspects of a memory, we will all naturally "remember" the details of a shared experience differently.

Similarly, what one pictures when asked to think of a library differs as well. To be sure, there are archetypical, stereotypical, and popular interpretations or assessments (based on simplified or standard conceptual projections of elements or conventions such as shelves, books, and reading desks), but while these are commonly accepted and associable symbols, simply providing them doesn't mean the desired subjective result will be the same (e.g., the cliché that a house does not make a home). The challenge then becomes how to find a common enough voice that still speaks to the individual without feeling homogenized or watered down. This process becomes more difficult when fundamental symbols associated with the library are then removed (or minimized) due to content digitization, such as the iconic books and shelves. What then are the common-thread connection points to which people can relate?

The misnomer in our reconceptualization of content is that while our physical selves lose a tactile connection point, content is not being lost but rather displaced. The digitization of content means we stand to gain a lot in terms of instantaneous access to articles or books that may otherwise have taken weeks to obtain physically (if we could even access them at all). The process of browsing the stacks is similarly displaced, as an absent or minimized physical collection means browsing content online instead. While unable to gratify or sate the empirical connection (environmental/behavioral/neurological/intellectual) made by physically browsing the stacks, digitization theoretically results in more efficient research as well as the exposed depth and breadth of related content.

In the wake of all this change, we may wonder, "What's left?" On a community level, the library reflects our personalities, pasts, and aspirations. The objective physical characteristics in the form archetypes (books, green shade lamps, quiet study areas, stacks, wood furniture) serve as the symbolic framework, while staff and the unique local voice evidenced in design, decoration, and services empirically and subjectively flesh out the library as a generator of emotional experience. The library has often, and for obvious reasons, become synonymous with reading and literacy, but the true definition of the library has always been ideological and transcendent of format: to inspire and facilitate learning, to advance knowledge, and to strengthen the community. In this, a library's space is different from that of a warehouse, as it has values, a philosophy, a spirit, and a soul. Not just a personalized space, it is personified as a lexicon of local culture and the human experience.

Praxis: Library 2025

What Didn't Happen . . .

To project our future library state by applying the generally accepted ergonomic design principle that if the extreme users (of a product, tool, or service) are identified then the middle or average user will be covered indirectly by approximation, we might define two extreme and opposite scenarios as Technophilic and Technophobic. The Technophilic extreme prefers the virtual mode of everything. All content "ethereally" located, the technological head leads the body. Chaos, in general, rules as technology governs decisions and we push for what we can do first, rather than cautiously considering priorities and outcomes. Great leaps are often made but there are dangerous falls, especially related to personal security. The library in this case either disappears or is reconceptualized to the point of being unrecognizable. Institutional libraries exist to a nominal extent but have largely become exaggerated cafés and convertible space without significance, while public libraries have lost funding and in many cases have become privatized.

Conversely, the Technophobic scenario is a reactionary approach to technology that expands upon the premise that our current state of technology has not delivered on its intention and that speaks to a relative digression of technology in some areas (such as social and privacy-invasive media) and reclamation in others (it created too much "noise" for research). This future considers the Internet as a failure in terms of negatively consuming our lives, exploding our privacy, and saturating our searches with comparatively little redeeming content. It views the current virtual state as a less-than-ideal landscape cluttered and overrun by consumerism, scams, and piracy—slum-like and more dangerous than unlit city streets. This scenario, while not wholly a return to nature, considers not just a rethinking but a complete overhauling of "the wheel." It views the virtual world, in contrast to our natural world, as a place where mistakes can be made and second chances exist.

In projecting these scenarios, I hyperbolize aspectual shifts to an irrational or allegorical end, completely out of balance with other conditional factors. In this case, I was favoring the technological with little consideration of our tangibly oriented subjective selves. Science fiction fascinates and holds didactic value for this very reason, as it presents and projects our current context of fears or concerns onto an instantaneous canvas of tomorrow, creating an alternative, typically dystopian universe where certain traits are magnified (as if they evolved in isolation of other societal factors and conditions). Was the future ever *not* chaotic, or maybe even pleasant? Projections of any future tend toward the technological while dismissing the physical, with its neurological, behavioral, and cognitive relationship to our environment. Library conjecture is certainly no different. Yet every day I see the two coexist, as they have evolved in balance and to a degree symbiotic, and I have no reason to believe the future will be different.

What Happened . . .

We breathed. Life happened gradually, as it does, and we realized the singularity wasn't, in all relativity, that near.* Potentialities of the modest future reveal a library that is more finely tuned to its patrons' needs and serves as a guiding voice of the community. Electronic books (*access to* not *ownership of*) dominate and patron-driven acquisition steers collection development. Print is still the preferred method for some materials, just as hard copy video is

---

* In his books *The Age of Spiritual Machines* (1999) and *The Singularity Is Near* (2005), Ray Kurzweil describes singularity as the ultimate symbiotic future state of humans balancing genetics, nanotechnology, and robotics. Among other things, this notion entails full-immersion virtual reality states (where we spend most of our lives), artificial intelligence/human hybrids, and the entire universe realized as a giant, highly efficient supercomputer.

still the delivery method of choice for the highest-quality effect and uncon-ditional performance (particularly in cinemas and in home theaters). Though bandwidth accommodation has improved exponentially, increased traffic and dynamic content traversing the Internet have made the streaming of Super HD 3D burdensome. In fact, though syncing of devices (where anyone can control everything with a smartphone and from anywhere) is de rigueur, sole proprietorship and digital rights management (DRM) have led to an equal opportunity à la carte access method environment. We've finally moved past our format monotheism, where only one delivery method can rule a time, to a more device-agnostic view where there is a time and a place for all.

In fact, because we are tactile and sensorial terrestrial creatures, we have a very physical interpretation of the digital age. Our high-tech devices coex-ist with antique furniture. And so our library environment is still centered on ergonomics and our behavioral response to space. "Locally sourced" has con-tinued to be a mantra in each community for its economic, ecologic, and cul-tural significance, and the library has become a vocal facilitator. The physical architecture, from materials to furniture to artwork, reflects this as much as programming, which has expanded to include things like community farms maintained by patrons, farmer's markets, studio spaces for fitness instruction, and kitchens for culinary and nutrition classes.

What is different about this library of the future is that it is wholly focused on what it alone can uniquely express to the community. Its services are cen-tered on its mission and it operates by the watchword "dialectal design." It doesn't worry about trying to do something it can't do better than somebody else. While library personnel roles shift and traditional responsibilities are con-stantly evolving, staff services parallel spatial relations as the biggest conduits for subjective impact and anchor patrons' emotional connections. It has long been quietly known that space is one of the more valuable assets of the library, but it is only now that the notion of a shelfless library has become liberating.

Just as the physical spaces will become multidimensional (in effect fleshed-out and activated Dewey fields), so too will the definition of content be further reconceptualized. Books, e-books, videos, and music are passive resources, and the library of the future will expand its definition of content to include programming and software. Graduating thus to *dynamic content* means that the library will provide not only quiet areas for study and meet-ings but also active spaces for learning how to use the programs and software provided, as well as to create and generate content. Dynamic content means creative spaces and *informing ability* through the provision of studios and labs outfitted with the resources, tools, and know-how (by librarians or commu-nity members). The librarians of the future find more of a natural home in this environment as the reaches of their abilities and training become enhanced. They maintain their positions as ambassadors of qualitative information and facilitators of the learning process. Just as print collections in the past were celebrated and promoted through book groups, displays, and programs, these more dynamic extensions of content embrace and explore the medium's potential.

References

Cornell University Library. 2010. *Report of the Collection Development Executive Committee Task Force on Print Collection Usage Cornell University Library.* http://staffweb .library.cornell.edu/system/files/CollectionUsageTF_ReportFinal11-22-10.pdf.

Kurzweil, Ray. 1999. *The Age of Spiritual Machines.* New York: Viking.

———. 2005. *The Singularity Is Near: When Humans Transcend Biology.* New York: Viking.

Pound, Ezra. 1916. *Gaudier-Brzeska.* New York: John Lane.

Schacter, Daniel. 1996. *Searching for Memory.* New York: Basic Books.

Stevens, Wallace. 1965. *The Necessary Angel: Essays on Reality and the Imagination.* New York: Vintage Books.

Zeisel, John. 2006. *Inquiry by Design.* New York: W. W. Norton.

Chapter 4

THE FACULTY COMMONS

Reimagining the Intellectual Heart of Campus

Krisellen Maloney

A large group of faculty stream out of the assembly room, many already engaged in conversation related to the new research findings just presented. They are headed to an adjacent area within the Faculty Commons where tables, booths, and other lounge-style seating are available for small group engagement and informal conversation. In the nearby kitchen area, a long counter offers platters of assorted cheeses, vegetables, fruits, and beverages to keep the conversations flowing. A quick look around other areas of the Faculty Commons shows that it is alive with activity. Humanities scholars are working with librarians to digitize and conduct textual analysis on a collection of manuscripts. Another faculty member is performing his final review of a new learning module that incorporates critical thinking skills into an assignment.

Tonight's event was organized by the Chemistry librarian. She has been involved with the aforementioned research project since its inception, which coincidentally occurred at an event much like the one that is taking place right now. Her connection? She had worked with the principal investigator on the Institutional Review Board for Human Subjects Research, where she had provided a literature review that saved the group time and also uncovered a paper that further focused the research topic. The librarian decided to host this event because she knew from conversations with the Social Science librarian that the policy issues implicit in the findings would be of great interest to Political Science faculty. Since she has regular meetings with the university's Research Office and is aware of an upcoming call for proposals for a large interdisciplinary research contract, she knew the groups should be talking. The Research Office is always eager to partner with the library on projects, seeing the library as neutral space perfect for connecting researchers from different disciplines. Plus, they know that investigators developing research proposals in the Faculty Commons will have support for literature reviews, experimental design, statistical analysis, and editing. In addition to expertise in data management, there is also support for other data-related services such as acquiring datasets and geographic information systems (GISs).

Does this scenario represent a realistic future for the library? Some will say yes; in fact, many of the roles and partnerships described are already taking place. Librarians have left the security of the reference desk and expanded their information expertise to take on new roles. Others will disagree; they worry about maintaining the library's existing services and question whether librarians should take on the range of roles described in the scenario. This tension between an outward view, focused on how best to serve the changing needs of the university, and an inward view, focused on how best to manage the library, has been a persistent theme in the library profession for decades.

For faculty, the value of the library is traditionally associated with access to information, although this increasingly takes place in offices and laboratories outside of the library building itself (Schonfeld and Housewright 2010). The diffusion of the library into the flow of faculty life—providing access to information and information-related services in classrooms, offices, and laboratories—is a welcome advancement to scholarship (Lougee 2002). The provision of a common space where faculty could regularly enjoy informal contact with one another could be of great use. Many of the issues they face today in teaching and research are too complex to be solved by a single person working in isolation. Yet in order to create an environment like the one described above, where the library and its services provide a platform for faculty success, new spaces will have to be created. More important, librarians will need to shift into new roles, and the faculty view of the library's role within the university will also have to change.

This chapter explores the evolution of spaces and services within library buildings, asking the question, "How can the library building as a physical space become a center for faculty life?" Lessons from past transitions, where the very concept of the library building changed, provide useful insights into how best to move forward.

The Evolution of Academic Library Buildings and Services

The educational function of the academic library is not a building. Yet the facility, representing as it does an approximation of the concept of the library, has a significant effect on the nature of its function and the priorities of its educational roles. (Reynolds 1973, 273)

When Reynolds wrote this in the early 1970s, the function of the library as a combination of services, resources, and spaces was self-evident. At the time, knowledge was represented in books, so library buildings and services were designed to acquire, protect, and provide access to that scarce resource. Librarians had the responsibility and the specialized knowledge necessary to build and organize a comprehensive collection that would meet all of the teaching and research needs of the campus. Because there was no other practical source, faculty and students had to visit the library building to access information.

The earliest academic library buildings were masterpieces of engineering. Because of the weight of the books, large, self-supporting book stacks, or stackwells, were produced to hold the institution's massive collections. Each floor of the stackwell was typically seven shelves or 7 feet 2 inches high and in the grandest libraries spanned several floors. Books were being published at a slow, predictable rate so formulas could be used to estimate the long-term size of the collection. To protect the books, stacks were closed and librarians facilitated access to materials. A main reading room typically sat adjacent to the stackwell and was a place of quiet solitude where readers independently absorbed themselves in the literature. Although the grandness of the historic reading room has become a symbol of a traditional academic library, its shape and enormity had a functional purpose. The buildings were designed in a period before electricity, and high ceilings (sometimes 30 to 40 feet high) were necessary for both natural light and air circulation. These massive structures and the completeness of the knowledge that they represented became the measure of the university (Ellsworth 1960).

The first big shift in the design of libraries came after World War II. The postwar growth in the demand for education flooded campuses with faculty and students from all walks of life whose expectations for access to information were different from those who had come before. Faculty and students were no longer satisfied with a mediated closed-stack system and became more interested in accessing the books directly. Although studying in isolation was still the accepted norm, faculty and student study habits began to shift. There was still a need for individual quiet space evidenced by the growing demand for faculty study rooms and carrels within the library. There was a simultaneous emerging demand for collaborative space such as group study rooms in which students could work together or with a faculty member. With all of these new requirements, the large reading room no longer supported the use patterns of the university community. Smaller spaces distributed through the building were needed.

The stackwells were also losing their utility. The safety issues associated with allowing faculty and students to access the stackwells—often several stories high and open in the center—were not the only problem. The volume of materials being published had exploded far beyond what planners had ever imagined. It was no longer possible to predict the growth of the print collection to build stackwells with appropriate capacity. The number of journals was also growing exponentially and new formats such as audiovisual materials and microforms were introduced. The rigid physical design of the stackwell could not be reconfigured to meet these changing needs. For the first time it was necessary to rethink the design of the library. The problem then, much like now, was not just redesigning a building but rather rethinking the services of the library to be responsive to the changing needs of the university.

We Are More Than Books Aren't We?

> Surely we have come far enough along in our thinking to know that it should be a "center for learning" in the same sense that it should be capable of housing and permitting the use of all kinds of carriers of knowledge, not just books, but all the things we class as audiovisual, and that it should be capable of housing all kinds of teaching and learning where it is essential that the student, the teacher and the material be present in one place at the same time. (Ellsworth 1960, 11)

From the postwar period to the beginning of the twenty-first century, the conditions described above brought about a fundamental change in libraries and the services they delivered. The days of perfectly organized closed stacks, the quiet solitude of the grand reading room, and the clearly defined role of the academic library within the university were gone. It was a difficult professional transition for many librarians, as rethinking library services challenged the very concept of the library and the professional identity of librarians. Librarians struggled to let go of the practices that had been effective in previous times and to develop new ones. The early years of this postwar transition found librarians attempting to recreate the orderly solitude of the original library in their new buildings. Even the shift from closed to open stacks and the introduction of browsing, one of the activities that today's faculty report to value most, presented concerns. Librarians worried that "open-access to the wide provision of library materials was the first sign of the supermarket, enabling users to browse freely . . . only to check out selected goods at the counters upon leaving" and that this would create a shallow understanding of the literature and cheapen the value of librarians' contribution to the academy (Reid-Smith 1985, 53).

The history of library buildings is often characterized as a trade-off between the need for collections storage space and the need for user study space (Ellsworth 1960; Shill and Tonner 2003). After World War II, new buildings were designed to be modular, but exponential increases in publication rates continued. As collections grew, the newly created study spaces were cannibalized to create more storage space. Although studies showed that approximately 40 percent of library users never used library materials, it was clear that some librarians considered the collection more important than user needs: "I am all for finding quietness for study but the library should be viewed as something other than a retreat from chaos in the dorm" (Boyer 1988, 8). Although new formats emerged, interior spaces and services continued to be optimized for printed formats. For example, microforms were tolerated but not given the same attention as print (Roselle 1982). There was also disagreement among librarians about whether nontraditional formats belonged in the library. When contemplating the appropriateness of audiovisual equipment and computer programs for library collections, for instance, librarians felt that the decision was "a philosophical question each institution will have to resolve for itself" (Snowball 1985, 99).

The late 1980s were grim years for libraries. Budgetary shortfalls were acknowledged to be long term and structural, not temporal. Rising journal costs and continued growth in publishing squeezed library budgets. Meanwhile, the digital revolution had begun: the card catalog was being replaced by an online public access catalog (OPAC), and the shift from print to online indexes was well under way. The first large, aggregated collections of journal content became available, and although it was not perceived as an existential threat at the time, it was suddenly possible to conduct limited library research from outside the library. The magnitude of these changes in scholarly communication was recognized as "a period roughly comparable to the introduction of the printed book" (Newman 1988, 173).

The influx of new students, many poorly prepared for college, created challenges for higher education (Brint 2009). Although there was a call for libraries to become more active in the teaching mission of the university they served, librarians were reluctant to do so. Budgets were already stretched as far as they could go, so library collections, the only practical source for academic information, remained the primary focus. The gap between the needs of the university and the services that libraries were willing to provide had become significant. The idea that faculty did not understand the value of the library frustrated some librarians, one of whom lamented that "the faculty want different things from libraries than librarians want from libraries" (Breivik and Wedgeworth 1988, 169). The collection, rather than the use of the collection, had defined the library. Their inward focus and the attachment to practices of the past caused a lack of support from the universities they served (Boyer 1988). Throughout this period library use declined. Librarians struggled to find ways to convince the universities of their value.

As is often the case, innovation arose from crisis. The confluence of several complex issues, including the growing size of the scholarly corpus, rapidly increasing automation, the emergence of born-digital content, and flat or decreasing funding levels drove the development of a new service model that would demonstrate value of the library to university administrators.

Students in the Library: From Adjustment to Transformation

> Students can learn in many ways, and campuses can create specific avenues to foster and recognize that learning. Some of the resulting learning environments will assuredly involve faculty members. But some will also involve librarians and student affairs staff, while others will harness community members and employers. These redesigned learning environments cannot be haphazard or unplanned in nature, but they can nevertheless be highly diverse. (Guskin 2003, 10)

The advent of the Information Commons in the early 1990s allowed librarians to adapt service offerings to the new computing-intensive environment. Library staff could work together with experts in technology to connect students with the information and tools they needed for their work. The utility of the space brought the students back into the library. Yet even as the Information Commons flourished, societal factors continued to increase pressure on universities. Students entering higher education in the late 1990s and early 2000s were less prepared than their predecessors. At the same time, their expectations for technology, communication, and engagement were increasing, and they struggled in what was to them the unfamiliar environment of university life. Federal and state governments had growing concerns about the quality and effectiveness of higher education and began to establish accountability measures tied to funding. Student learning had become a major issue for many universities, and finding better ways to provide academic support was an important priority. Although the Information Commons represented a partnership with campus computing centers, its focus was typically an extension of traditional library service.

The success realized with this partnership served as the inspiration for the next phase of library evolution, the Learning Commons. The Learning Commons moved beyond providing the technology and support necessary for library-related work, bringing together academic and student support units from around campus to create an entirely new space. Librarians expanded their skills and forged partnerships with units such as the writing center, tutoring, orientation, and career services to create a seamless learning environment. Libraries reshaped their spaces and services to answer a crucial university need and administrators took notice, responding with increased resources. In the period between 1995 and 2002, most large-scale library renovation projects included an Information Commons or Learning Commons, and user space within the library was given equal weight with collection space (Shill and Tonner 2003). Librarians leveraged their new expertise by teaching information literacy, responding to research questions, and collaborating on collection-sharing projects to solve real issues facing higher education.

The success of the Learning Commons demonstrates that providing physical spaces that connect people with each other and with the resources and services they need creates an environment that is greater than the sum of its parts. While the value of the Learning Commons to the university in terms of student engagement, which is known to be a primary factor in student persistence and graduation, cannot be easily or quickly quantified (Oakleaf 2010), measures are being explored and developed to better demonstrate the strengths and weaknesses of libraries' new services. The emergent properties of the space—the new connections between students, librarians, tutors, and instructors, the leveraging of the strengths of the partners, and the resulting engagement with and among students—create an excitement that is difficult to dismiss. Not only did the Learning Commons bring students back to the library, but it helped to solve a problem for the university. By successfully transforming themselves in a period of less than 20 years and adapting to the changing needs of students, libraries shifted once again to the center of student life. Is it possible to take what we have learned from tackling this university issue in order to create a similar platform for faculty?

The Library as a Platform for Faculty Innovation

Platform building is, by definition, a kind of exercise in emergent behavior. . . . The beaver builds a dam to better protect itself against its predators, but that engineering has the emergent effect of creating a space where kingfishers and dragonflies and beetles can make a life for themselves. (Johnson 2010, 182–83)

This broad view of platforms as the substrate that simultaneously focuses and encourages activity provides the foundation for the concept of the Faculty Commons. Platforms include coffee shops, cafeterias, shared workspaces, and group meeting areas. Any space that draws people with ideas together and allows for conversation and connections can be a platform for innovation. Platforms also encourage reuse and recycling of existing component parts, where ideas, solutions, services, and resources are used in different arrangements. Many of the most important innovations of our time took root and blossomed in environments like these where people from different backgrounds saw problems and possibilities through different lenses.

Libraries have the potential to create platforms that encourage faculty connections, efficiency, and effectiveness by drawing on lessons from the past. The progression of the concept of library as place, from a grand storehouse for collections to an integrated learning environment for students, shows that when three key factors come together, the library can successfully redefine itself:

- *Connect services to the mission of the university.* Universities are facing challenges that will require focused, creative, and collaborative action to address. As a neutral space with multidisciplinary expertise, the library is in the ideal position to build cross-disciplinary relationships and create spaces to support the changing mission. To fully embrace this role, it will be necessary to look broadly and do what is needed within the university. The most difficult times for libraries have resulted when the goals of the library were not aligned with the goals of the university.
- *Embrace new job descriptions.* To capitalize on this opportunity, librarians must "reconceptualize their expertise, skills, and roles in the context of institutional mission, not traditional library functions alone" (Simmons-Welburn, Donovan, and Bender 2008, 132). This has been done before. Librarians evolved from their singular role as keepers of books and are now woven into university life, providing services within laboratories and classrooms.
- *Partner to provide a critical mass of services.* The success of the Learning Commons is due in part to centralizing the expertise students seek at the point of need. Through years of partnering

to build and share collections, librarians have gained significant expertise in building collaborative relationships.

With these three key factors in mind, libraries can turn to developing a platform that supports the evolving needs of faculty.

In its most basic form, the Faculty Commons extends traditional library services to the digital environment, including scanning of special collections and integration of information literacy online modules into the curriculum. A parallel can be drawn here with the Information Commons. Much as the Information Commons evolved into the Learning Commons, libraries must evolve the ways they offer these services to increase their value to faculty. There are several initiatives under way in academic libraries to create Faculty Commons, but they have thus far met with mixed success (Bell 2011).

Creating change that is truly transformative will require that we think beyond what we can do alone and create strong partnerships, perhaps co-locating services from other university units in the Faculty Commons space. Because faculty already have spaces to work in isolation, the Faculty Commons should provide spaces and services that connect people. The facility needs a variety of different rooms, furniture configurations, and tools that encourage and support different kinds of interaction, including group study rooms with whiteboards and display monitors, interactive classrooms, and collaborative learning environments to facilitate shared development of content.

A Focus on Teaching and Research

[W]e now know that more than 50 percent of the students starting college with a stated desire to major in science or engineering drop out of those majors before graduating. We can no longer blame this problem entirely on the nation's high schools. A substantial body of research demonstrates conclusively that the problem is frequently caused by poor undergraduate teaching in physics, chemistry, biology, math, and engineering, particularly in the freshman and sophomore years. (Rawlins 2012)

This recent statement by the president of the Association of American Universities underscores the issues facing universities. The same student characteristics that drove the creation of the Learning Commons, including lack of preparedness and high expectations of engagement and communication, also come into play in the classroom. The success of the university requires teaching students more effectively and providing them with the skills they need for their future. While the need to transform higher education is great, most of today's faculty have never received formal instruction in teaching methods (Brint 2009). There is a need for universities to provide avenues for faculty members to adapt and enhance their teaching practices in this environment.

Furthermore, the increasing expectations on the part of universities for faculty to seek research funding, combined with the increased requirements by funding agents for interdisciplinary research, make it more important than ever for faculty to collaborate. Current boundaries between and among disciplines are largely the result of university administrative structures to support research and teaching as well as the nature of professional societies in the first half of the last century. Many of the support structures within the university will have to change to encourage new relationships among faculty across departmental, college, and discipline boundaries. One of the overarching themes in facilitating interdisciplinary research is finding ways to bring together faculty who would not otherwise meet. Libraries' current state of knowledge of advanced storage, processing, and communication technologies provides a means for tackling difficult problems spanning multiple knowledge domains.

Responding to this, a Faculty Commons could organize workshops and services covering common ground for faculty across disciplines, ranging from learning theories to grant writing and citation management. Practice-based workshops on using information resources in the classroom, using advanced features of the course management system, and introducing technology to the classroom are of value to faculty from all disciplines. Faculty could receive syllabus consultations and feedback on lesson design. Support could be provided to develop informal mentoring systems, allowing faculty to share, critique, and modify modules that they have found or created. A host of services related to digital or institutional repositories could complement this mix, including project consultation, digitization, and metadata creation. Additional offerings could include support for digital humanities, the acquisition and storage of datasets, and statistical and GIS feedback. Consultation services could be provided for faculty on using copyright works and managing their own intellectual property. Partners for these services could include teaching and learning centers and academic technology units. The synergistic opportunities to be found in a Faculty Commons are endless.

Spaces That Are Greater Than the Sum of Their Parts

[I]nnovation prospers when ideas can serendipitously connect and recombine with other ideas, when hunches can stumble across other hunches that successfully fill in their blanks. (Johnson 2010, 123)

The services provided within the Faculty Commons will surely evolve based on experience and with the changing needs of the university. To the extent possible, spaces should be general rather than specialized. Each university will have unique needs. Some universities have existing support infrastructure for teaching; others have strong support for interdisciplinary research. To recognize opportunities, librarians will have to explore the drivers of change and the needs of faculty at their institution to uncover the potential of the Faculty Commons. One indicator of a successful Faculty Commons is the presence of frequent, informal face-to-face communication between peers in lounge areas. Because of the lack of structure inherent in the task, it may be the most difficult space to create. There is some evidence, however, that faculty are ready to move in this direction. A recent study found that younger and newer faculty were more likely to use the physical space of the library for study, work, or relaxation without using library resources during their visit (Antell and Engel 2006). As the students of 2000 become the faculty of today, libraries can provide an appealing place to work or relax among colleagues.

Libraries have evolved over the years to remain central to academic life. Spaces and services that we now see as core to the library were not always so. The past 50 years have shown what it means to connect students and faculty with the information they need. The optimal means to organize, store, and preserve content has changed, and so has the allocation of library spaces. There is an abundance of evidence that indicates that learning and innovation occur when people connect, share physical spaces, and exchange ideas. With the Faculty Commons, libraries have the opportunity to continue their evolution by creating spaces that enable and empower faculty to move forward in an ever-changing information environment.

References

Antell, K., and D. Engel. 2006. "Conduciveness to Scholarship: The Essence of Academic Library as Place." *College and Research Libraries* 67, no. 6: 536–60.

Bell, S. J. 2011. "Bringing Back the Faculty: The Evolution of the Faculty Commons in the Library." *Library Issues: Briefings for Faculty and Administrators* 31, no. 4. www.libraryissues.com/pub/PDF3104Mar2011.pdf.

Boyer, E. L. 1988. "Connectivity." In *Libraries and the Search for Academic Excellence*, edited by P. S. Breivik and R. Wedgeworth, 3–11. Metuchen, NJ: Scarecrow Press.

Breivik, P. S., and R. Wedgeworth. 1988. "Strategies for Improved Use of Libraries in Support of Academic Excellence—Summary of Panel Discussion." In *Libraries and the Search for Academic Excellence*, edited by P. S. Breivik and R. Wedgeworth, 169–72. Metuchen, NJ: Scarecrow Press.

Brint, S. 2009. *The Academic Devolution? Movements to Reform Teaching and Learning in US Colleges and Universities, 1985–2010*. Center for Studies in Higher Education Research and Occasional Paper Series: CSHE.12.9. Berkeley, CA: University of California, Berkeley.

Ellsworth, R. E. 1960. *Planning the College and University Library Building: A Book for Campus Planners and Architects*. Boulder, CO: Pruett Press.

Guskin, A. E. M. M. B. 2003. "Dealing with the Future NOW." *Change* 35, no. 4: 10.

Johnson, S. 2010. *Where Good Ideas Come From: The Natural History of Innovation*. New York: Riverhead Books.

Lougee, W. P. 2002. *Diffuse Libraries: Emergent Roles for the Research Library in the Digital Age*. Washington, DC: Council on Library and Information Resources.

National Academy of Sciences, National Academy of Engineering and Institute of Medicine. 2005. *Facilitating Interdisciplinary Research*. Washington, DC: National Academies Press.

Newman, F. 1988. "Academic Libraries and the American Resurgence." In *Libraries and the Search for Academic Excellence*, edited by P. S. Breivik and R. Wedgeworth, 173–86. Metuchen, NJ: Scarecrow Press.

Oakleaf, M. 2010. *The Value of Academic Libraries: A Comprehensive Research Review and Report*. Chicago: Association of College and Research Libraries.

Rawlins, H. R. 2012. "Why Research Universities Must Change." *Inside Higher Ed* (blog), March 30 (3:00 a.m.). www.insidehighered.com/views/2012/03/30/essay-research-universities-must-pay-more-attention-student-learning.

Reid-Smith, E. R. 1985. "The Concept of Informatacy in Academic Libraries: Some Aspects of Self-Service." In *Issues in Academic Librarianship: Views and Case Studies for the 1980s and 1990s*, edited by P. Spyers-Duran and T. W. Mann Jr., 52–62. Westport, CT: Greenwood Press.

Reynolds, M. M., ed. 1973. *Reader in the Academic Library. Readers*. Washington, DC: Microcard Editions.

Roselle, W. C. 1982. "The Microforms Facility at the Golda Meir Library of the University of Wisconsin–Milwaukee." In *Advances in Library Administration and Organization*, edited by G. B. McCabe, B. Kreissman, and W. C. Jackson, 1. Greenwich, CT: JAI Press.

Schonfeld, R. C., and R. Housewright. 2010. *Faculty Survey 2009: Key Strategic Insights for Libraries, Publishers, and Societies*. New York: Ithaka S+R.

Shill, H. B., and S. Tonner 2003. "Creating a Better Place: Physical Improvements in Academic Libraries, 1995–2002." *College and Research Libraries* 64, no. 6: 431–66.

Simmons-Welburn, J., G. Donovan, and L. Bender. 2008. "Transforming the Library: The Case for Libraries to End Incremental Measures and Solve Problems for Their Campuses Now." *Library Administration and Management* 22, no. 3: 5.

Snowball, G. C. 1985. "Library Buildings for the Twenty-first Century: A Planning Issue for the 1980s." In *Issues in Academic Librarianships: Views and Case Studies for the 1980s and 1990s*, edited by P. Spyers-Duran and T. W. Mann Jr., 93–9. Westport, CT: Greenwood Press.

Chapter 5

FREE-RANGE LIBRARIANSHIP

Public Librarian as Park Ranger

Hugh Rundle

The future for public libraries lies in the services we offer rather than the collections we hold. When everyone has the Internet in their pocket, library services will be about discovery and understanding in a world of information and cultural abundance, rather than the past emphasis on the storage and sharing of scarce information and cultural artifacts. Up until now, librarians have worked in libraries because that was where the world's information and knowledge were stored. Yet in just a couple of decades we have gone from collecting content and providing services in a physical location to making content available and providing limited services remotely. Such a change requires a radical rethinking of the role of libraries and librarians. Now that information is available anywhere Internet access can be found, librarians can provide services wherever they are needed. The key to the future of quality librarianship is to take the next bold step: when the library is anywhere, librarians should be everywhere.

The Internet's rise over the past 20 years from a niche academic tool to a ubiquitous aspect of billions of people's lives has profoundly changed our relationship with information. Libraries generally have been quick to see the advantages of sharing information and providing services online. When the World Wide Web appeared, suddenly we had the ability to provide access to index services and library catalogs remotely via the web. More recently, the move toward Library 2.0 has enabled patrons of many academic and public libraries to "Ask a Librarian" using online chat or to undertake a quick reference inquiry through social media. With the rise of powerful mobile computing devices like smartphones and tablets, we now boast that the library can be anywhere; there is even a "Library Anywhere" mobile application.

When it comes to public libraries, however, the literature and the overwhelming majority of library services remain focused on the physical library.

Some libraries are removing their reference desks and using tablet computers to provide roving reference services (Juntumaa 2011), which enables librarians to assist patrons in a more approachable manner at the point of need, but it still requires those patrons to be located within the library building. While *American Libraries* was editorializing on the wonders of telecommuting as early as 2000, this was only in the context of librarians working remotely from home (Schneider 2000). Providing online databases, instant chat, and mobile-friendly catalogs broadens the library's reach beyond its walls, but these services still rely on the patron taking the initiative to go to the library, either physically or virtually. The library may be anywhere, but librarians are still living and working within the walls of their buildings.

This being the case, libraries end up in direct competition with Google and other search engines. Given Google's size, resources, and head start in online search services, this is a contest that municipal libraries cannot possibly hope to win. If we simply put our resource-finding tools on the web and hope for the best, libraries and the communities they serve will lose out. The information that is *probably correct* and *convenient* will always trump the information that is *more complete and reliable* but *inconvenient* to access (Dubicki 2010). The truth is that few individuals think to ask a librarian when they can just ask Google (Stephens 2011). To avoid the results of such competition with Google and its contemporaries, public libraries need to adopt and expand traditional outreach programs and newer embedded service models used by some academic and special libraries to build an entirely new type of library service.

Building a Model of "Everywhere"

Traditional models for extending library service outside the library have been outreach projects in which a librarian travels to places outside the library for a short time frame and provides limited library services. For instance, bookmobiles expand local library services, as do librarians who visit prison and detention centers. These are worthwhile services, but even the very best outreach service today is still predicated on the assumption that the real action is back at the physical library. These efforts are often about marketing as much as librarianship; they are an optional extra to be provided when funding allows. Emily Ford (2009) dares to suggest that "outreach is (un)dead" because many things generally considered to be outreach should more rightly be considered core library operations. Ford may be underselling these zombies, however. What might traditionally be seen as outreach may well become the core mission of many libraries in the future as we combine the power of the Internet with the local knowledge and skills of librarians.

Librarians, of course, do much more than simply store and provide access to information. As illuminated by an effective reference interview, good librarians help people understand and decide what it is they are actually seeking. Best of all, good librarians help people find things they didn't even know they needed. To do this well, we need to have face-to-face interaction with patrons. Instead of simply providing online access to information, librarians should be placed at the physical point of need, with online tools at hand. We can now move from remotely accessed content and services to content accessed remotely through face-to-face services.

In many cases, the point of need will still be the physical library where students and independent learners study and collaborate. The library will continue to be an important place for librarians to employ their skills, but in recent years some libraries have been experimenting with embedding librarians in other spaces. Embedded librarians are sent to the point of need to bring services to patrons, which frees patrons from the need to come to the library. Thus we have librarians physically embedded in laboratories, newsrooms, and other research facilities, and virtually embedded in online course management systems for programs or individuals classes. Embedding librarians allows them to work within the context of the information need, on the fly. Just by being there the librarian is able to make connections, find relevant research results, and help patrons make sense of data.

Shumaker (2009) gives the four examples of Fairfax Media, Penn State University, Mitre Corporation, and the University of Sheffield. Fairfax, a major Australian newspaper publisher, downsized their physical library and relocated librarians into general office space with journalists. This caused librarians and journalists to work more closely together, which both groups found even more valuable. When a larger library space became possible again, staff declined the offer to return. At Penn State, a librarian attended every class of the first-year "Effective Speech" course so that he was available to assist students while they were in class and thereby build a relationship that would last their whole campus career. Mitre Corporation moved one of their librarians from the library to work with staff from the main departmental customer of the library, attending meetings and consultations. Finally, the University of Sheffield moved librarians into the hospital to assist student nurses with information searches rather than leave them in the library waiting for nurses to come to them. There are five factors common to the success of these embedded librarian models that will be discussed in more detail in this chapter: (1) guidance, (2) personalization, (3) proximity, (4) visibility, and (5) context.

For public libraries the opportunities seem more daunting, since unlike academic or special libraries they do not have an annual, reliable intake of users with easily definable needs. Nor do their patrons work in easily defined spaces within the same organization. Public library users can appear at any time, from anywhere, and with any sort of query. This makes it much harder to determine what an embedded model might look like for such a wide range of users. Public librarians would, in a sense, be "de-embedded": released from the library into the community. For public libraries, it makes more sense to talk not of embedded librarianship but rather of "free-range" librarianship. Luckily, there is already a model in place for how free-range public library services might work: the park ranger.

Park Rangers and the Information Ecosystem

National parks in many nations employ park rangers to perform a wide range of tasks required to care for and educate the public about unique places. Park rangers can be found at the entrance points for national and state parks, advising visitors and accepting entry and camping fees. As their name implies, however, park rangers also spend a great deal of time traveling through the parks maintaining trails, campgrounds, and huts, assisting hikers who are in trouble, providing tours, educating visitors about the plants and animals that live in the park, conducting research, and protecting the health of the park. Park rangers assist visitors at the point of need rather than sitting around waiting for people to come to them with questions. They are a constructive model for free-range librarianship because the tasks they perform fit the five factors common to embedded librarianship. Furthermore, their work requires them to move through a landscape on a daily basis assisting people at their point of need.

Factor One: Guidance

Like national parks, the world of information contains an abundance of wonders, often spread over hundreds, thousands, or millions of sites (both physical and virtual). People already have almost instant access to vastly more information than can ever fit inside a library building, but for them to truly appreciate these wonders they need a guide or, at the very least, a map. Just as park rangers maintain walking trails, bridges, and signs, librarians assist community members in finding their way through the abundance of information and misinformation. Some of this work is simply a matter of guiding patrons toward what we consider the safest and most beautiful routes to information. At other times it means sitting down with them as they contemplate a crossroads, figuring out what they hope to find and advising them accordingly. It might also mean noticing where they are heading and providing some advice on what to expect or, where conditions may be troubled, suggesting an alternative route.

Factor Two: Personalization

Park rangers provide advice and assistance specific to each party of visitors based on their assessment of the group's fitness, equipment, and goals. Librarians assist members of the public, local business owners, students, and others with their own specific needs. Sometimes they will be able to assist on the spot, while at other times they will need to conduct further research and respond to the individual the next day with a considered list of sources, books, or ideas.

One of the few existing examples of the park ranger in practice in librarianship is Alain de Botton's School of Life in London. One of the school's programs, "Bibliotherapy," is a service in which clients describe their book preferences and reading habits and a "bibliotherapist" makes recommendations (a few titles immediately and an expanded list within a couple of days) for what they should read next. The service is focused on fiction but includes some philosophical and classical texts. Bibliotherapy is an important example of personalized services for modern public libraries: it is designed for people who feel overwhelmed by their reading options and offers guidance amid abundance. It is also highly personalized, as clients make an appointment in advance and receive a personalized "prescription." While at its essence bibliotherapy is a classic example of reader's advisory, it also leverages the ability to provide such a service anywhere by downloading e-books to the client's device on the spot.

Factor Three: Proximity

Park rangers are not just available through a website or phone line. Most of their work guiding, educating, and assisting the public is done face-to-face as they travel through their park. The value of face-to-face contact in solving problems, sharing ideas, and understanding people's real needs is well established (Purdy 2011; Siegal 2012). Recent research suggests that face-to-face reference and information assistance is not just valuable but also the model preferred by most library patrons, even young undergraduate students (Sobel 2009). Free-range librarianship will see librarians providing face-to-face contact in multiple public places and, possibly, on house calls to people's own homes.

Factor Four: Visibility

Park rangers wear uniforms as a visible sign of their position so that it is easy to spot them and ask for assistance. Visibility will be important for free-range librarians so that all members of the community are aware of library services. Librarians can ensure that they are physically visible by wearing some kind of identifier, whether a uniform, badge, or other item. Librarians can also make themselves more virtually visible by using geolocation services like Foursquare, "checking in" as they visit particular places or events. Librarians will also need to improve their social visibility by cultivating relationships with key people and organizations, such as local journalists, influential business owners, and other public-facing government agencies.

Factor Five: Context

The most important thing about free-range librarianship is that it provides in-context, real-time assistance. Park rangers do this every day, assisting visitors in finding their way, identifying a unique local species, or understanding the ecology of the area they are visiting. Free-range librarians, untethered from the library building, will be able to assist the shop owner inside his or her own business, help the local historian on the site of the building being researched, and guide the independent researcher in using the resources available in his or her own home office.

A Day in the Life of a Free-Range Librarian

Let's consider how a free-range librarian might spend her day. It begins at 8:00 a.m. in the local café, where she checks in using various social media tools before compiling some reading recommendations for a patron she spoke to the previous day. The sticker on her laptop and the badge on her blouse inspire a café customer stopping in for his morning coffee to ask her for help in locating a particular tax form. She spends the next couple of hours completing some research recommendations for the mayor before heading to the Men's Shed to have a chat with those gathered there. They don't need any help today, but during last week's visit she offered reading recommendations to several of them so they discuss which books they have enjoyed since her last visit. Next she attends a meeting with the Parks Department at City Hall. She makes a note of the grass species they are trying out on the new sports field so that she can look later for any research papers of similar trials that might provide Parks Department representatives with greater insight. While at City Hall she bumps into a friend from the City Planning Department who mentions she is working on a new parking scenario for a local shopping strip. The librarian now heads to the local mosque, where she makes friendly conversation with a few individuals after afternoon prayers. One woman asks for advice on whom to contact about an immigration matter, and another requests assistance in locating some Persian poetry e-books. Next, she walks with a local baker to the Traders Association meeting, where she mentions the discussion she had with the planner about the parking idea and gives a presentation on the augmented reality application one of her colleagues has been working on to enable visitors to see what each shop looked like in the past. Five o'clock already? Our librarian has spent the day providing library services and assisting people in finding information and literature—all without setting foot in a building called "the library."

A Free-Range Librarianship Model

The emergence of a free-range library model will bring with it opportunities and risks. There will be risks to funding, political support, and professional standards, but the first and most important risk is poor implementation. The free-range model is not a matter of simply transplanting librarians from a desk in the library to a table elsewhere in the public realm. Free-range librarianship is about anticipating situations in which people will desire assistance from an information professional and ensuring that a librarian is available in person at the time of need. This may mean attending conventions and fairs or visiting schools, workplaces, and clubhouses. It may mean operating from coworking spaces with a "please interrupt me" sign and assisting people face-to-face in between working on online projects. Whatever the case, it will need to be implemented carefully and directed by the needs and desires of the particular community.

Funding and Political Support

Free-range librarianship will both require and result naturally from a shift in focus from collection development and maintenance to discovery and education. This will see public lending libraries reduce the resources they put toward developing general collections of physical items and transition into a more organic, patron-driven acquisitions model similar to those many academic libraries have recently begun employing (Swords 2011). Continued growth in e-books is likely, further pushing librarians toward a more proactive service model, since patrons will no longer need to physically visit the library in order to borrow books (Pew Internet and American Life Project 2012). As librarians increasingly work with people in their own space, we may well see an increasing focus on assisting people in assessing information sources themselves. Community members may come to see librarians as personal information advisors and coaches rather than simply the person who knows where the latest bestseller is shelved.

A consequence of the move away from collection development toward online curation, information assessment, and information literacy education may be the repurposing of library buildings. A reduction in the amount of room needed to physically house books and other items will enable library spaces to be used for other information and literature-related purposes. This may be as places for coworking and performance, or as places to share ideas via discussion groups and talks rather than through circulating written works. An example of what libraries in 2025 might look like is the Wheeler Centre in Melbourne, Australia. Opened at the same time as Melbourne's bid to become the second UNESCO City of Literature, the Wheeler Centre is a collection of writer's spaces, meeting rooms, offices, and an auditorium. The Centre hosts live-streamed lunchtime lectures, unconferences, and author talks. Libraries in 2025 are likely to concentrate more on these types of spaces that foster the creation and sharing of ideas rather than the storage and organization of physical items.

This has profound political consequences for the funding and support of public libraries. Traditionally, libraries have been evaluated based on the size and quality of their collections, the number of visitors, and for lending libraries the number of loans. A free-range library model is by its nature incapable of measuring any of these things. Indeed, such measurements make little sense in this context. With a variety of sources of literature and quality information available for free online, free-range librarianship taken to the extreme need not even involve a collection provided by the library itself, whether physical or digital. However, if the organizations funding public libraries cannot point to a physical collection, it may become politically difficult for them to justify funding library services. The library becomes invisible just as it becomes more relevant to a changed information landscape (Bosanquet 2010; Scheinfeldt 2012).

This has the potential to create a downward spiral in which communities insist on keeping the physical trappings of a library, thus preventing their limited dollars from being spent on innovative services more suited to their needs in the modern, connected world. While recent renovation plans for the New York Public Library (Sherman 2011) and the Library of Birmingham (Jeffries 2010) show it is possible to gain management and community support for redesigned library spaces and services, the 2011 Parliamentary Inquiry into school libraries and teacher librarians in Australian schools (Parliament of Australia 2011) reveals how politicians and funding bodies will strongly support investment in physical spaces without understanding what is needed to modernize a library. The Inquiry found that while the Australian government had invested heavily in new school library buildings, many schools were without teacher librarians to staff them. This example of focusing on the outward trappings of libraries at the expense of actual library services is likely to continue.

Managing the political ramifications of a shift to free-range librarianship will be crucial to its success. History is littered with examples of resistance to change, and particularly changes to treasured cultural institutions. For library managers attempting to facilitate these changes, it will be important to spell out exactly what they are hoping to achieve, why the change is necessary, and what benefits the community will see. This will require an adjustment in the metrics used to measure success, something library managers and directors have recently started to consider (Miller 2012). It becomes more difficult to measure the library's value to society when it moves to a service model in which there is nothing to physically share, and there are no assets, no fees, and no formal qualifications for clients. Studies such as the Fels Institute of Government's study into the economic value of the Free Library of Philadelphia (Fels Research and Consulting 2010) or the Dollars and Sense study commissioned by the Public Libraries Victoria Network (SGS Economics and Planning 2011) go some way toward measuring the less tangible value of library services, but large in-depth studies like these are not likely to occur with any frequency. The approach of the New Economics Foundation (Hawk, n.d.) in attempting to measure "social return on investment" is more promising, with the Foundation attempting to develop standards for measuring the economic and social impact of less tangible and direct impacts from government programs and services.

The Internet and the Digital Divide

Free-range librarianship requires librarians and the community members they assist to access information and literature quickly from wherever they are and to provide a full library service experience outside of the library building. While the rise of the Internet and mobile computing is what makes free-range librarianship possible, it is still possible only in certain places. In Manhattan or central Melbourne these technologies are omnipresent, but in remote and rural communities it will be much harder, if not impossible, to pursue this model. Projects like Australia's ambitious National Broadband Network

(NBN) (Commonwealth of Australia, n.d.) will assist with this, but even the NBN will not necessarily ensure widespread *wireless* Internet access.

In large countries with dispersed populations such as the United States and Australia, librarians must be mindful of the rural-city divide and what free-range librarianship might mean for rural library services. On the one hand, rural library services are already comfortable with the idea of providing some library services outside of the library building, as mobile libraries have been operating for decades to dispersed populations, using everything from donkeys to boats to extend the library's service area (Benstead, Spacey, and Goulding 2004). With this background, some of the potential issues around managing dispersed staff and providing extended services are already being dealt with by rural libraries. On the other hand, rural areas on the whole have notoriously poor Internet access (Belson 2006), making it extremely difficult to provide a type of library service that requires fast wireless Internet. While in Australia (via the NBN) and the UK (UK Department for Culture, Media and Sport 2010) national, government-backed broadband networks are planned to be rolled out to every town, this is not the case in all countries.

Professional Skills and Management

The personal mobile computing device will very likely be the primary information tool in 2025, with 47 percent of all Internet connections in Australia already occurring via mobile devices (Australian Bureau of Statistics 2012). Librarians without a widespread knowledge of and competence in using a wide variety of devices and platforms will simply be unable to perform the job of a free-range librarian. Such technical knowledge will be a core requirement of all such positions. Librarians will need to use a variety of devices, operating systems, applications, and formats. This may involve using the library services' device, a personal device, or a client's device. Furthermore, without the ability to call upon a familiar physical collection or other staff, it will not be enough to be simply competent: free-range librarians will need to be uniformly excellent at their job. The quality of this service will have a lasting effect on the public perception of the library service, for better or worse.

Library and Information Science education will need to be up to the task, as will professional development programs for librarians already in the profession. Strength in traditional skills such as reference interviews and a deep knowledge of literature will be prized, but only in combination with a sophisticated understanding of information technology, strong search skills, and above all an ability to connect with people and develop relationships with community groups and individuals.

While they will need to excel, librarians working individually in the community are difficult to supervise. Questions will need to be answered about how to measure performance and ensure that librarians are actually doing the job for which they are paid. This may see libraries move to different ways of assessing staff performance. The other side of the performance management coin is professional development and service coordination. Librarians operating separately from each other will need ways to ensure that they collaborate regularly to assist coordination of effort, development of further service innovations, and for training purposes. Regular team meetings, either physical or virtual, will be necessary to ensure consistency of service and vision. All of these things need to be considered when moving to a model of dispersed service and therefore dispersed staff.

These changes all mean that we are likely to see a major change in the way library services are managed and staffed. As roles disappear and merge, flatter structures are likely to replace traditional, hierarchical arrangements of lower-skilled library clerks supporting librarians, who in turn are supervised by one or more layers of senior librarians. Without physical circulating collections, many of the simple transactional roles will be rendered obsolete. At the same time, with the librarians' role now moving to a more highly skilled and largely autonomous and mobile role, we may see a move toward a management structure akin to a general practice medical clinic, where doctors act as a board of management for the clinic but operate in many ways more as cotenants, each with his or her own patient list.

Finally, dispersed service suggests a rethinking of the concept of "opening hours." As Gosford Library Service found, providing services at the place and time that is most convenient for your clients (or potential clients) may mean starting work at 5:30 a.m. (Flores 2002). Providing in-person service at a night game of cricket, baseball, or football might mean a 10:00 p.m. or later finish. These scenarios will lead to new discussions about core hours, overtime pay, and family-friendly schedules, and will involve different needs and trade-offs for different services.

Conclusion

Despite doomsayers declaring the death of libraries (Coffman 2012), the future for librarianship is full of promise. While there will be challenges, there are also great opportunities. As virtual space and real space become more and more entwined, the skills of librarianship will be needed more, not less. If we choose to use our new, powerful information tools to make library services more relevant, more personal, and more useful to people, libraries and the communities they serve will flourish. By seizing the opportunities already available to us, librarians can find new, richer, and more effective ways to help communities prosper intellectually, physically, socially, and economically.

We can ensure our future by successfully engaging with the complex questions of how our library services are operated and funded, and by exploring the park ranger model of free-range librarianship. This is a librarianship that provides guidance amid abundance, helping our communities to find the quality information and cultural works they need from the millions of options available to them. It is a librarianship that genuinely engages patrons on a personal level, providing information and assistance tailored to their particular needs and abilities. It is a librarianship that uses the power of wireless and mobile technology not just to get out from behind the desk but to get out of the building and make face-to-face contact with patrons on their own territory. And it is a librarianship that proudly makes itself visible in physical space with badges and signage, and in virtual space with check-ins and posts. Free-range librarians walk confidently through the information landscape just as park rangers rove their parks, providing truly valuable, in-context, real-time guidance, advice, and companionship to those on the trails.

References

Australian Bureau of Statistics. 2012. "Type of Access Connection." *8153.0—Internet Activity, Australia*, December 2011. www.abs.gov.au/ausstats/abs@.nsf/Lookup/8153.0Chapter3Dec%202011.

Belson, Ken. 2006. "Rural Areas Left Out in Slow Lane of High-Speed Data Highway." *New York Times*, September 28. www.nytimes.com/2006/09/28/technology/28vermont.html?pagewanted=all&_r=0.

Benstead, Kerry, Rachel Spacey, and Anne Goulding. 2004. "Changing Public Library Service Delivery to Rural Communities in England." *New Library World* 105, no. 11: 400–409.

Bosanquet, Lyn. 2010. "Building Relevance amidst the Content Revolution." *Library Management* 31, no. 3: 133–44.

Coffman, Steve. 2012. "The Decline and Fall of the Library Empire." *Searcher* 20, no. 3 (April). www.infotoday.com/searcher/apr12/Coffman-The-Decline-and-Fall-of-the-Library-Empire.shtml.

Commonwealth of Australia, Department of Broadband, Communications and the Digital Economy. n.d. NBN—National Broadband Network. www.nbn.gov.au.

Dubicki, Eleonora. 2010. "Research Behavior Patterns of Business Students." *Reference Services Review* 38, no. 3: 360–84.

Fels Research and Consulting. 2010. *The Economic Value of the Free Library in Philadelphia*. Philadelphia: Fels Research and Consulting.

Flores, Alan. 2002. "Book Express: A Mini-Library for Rail Commuters." *New Library World* 103, no. 7: 272.

Ford, Emily. 2009. "Outreach is (un)Dead." *In the Library with the Lead Pipe*. www.inthelibrarywiththeleadpipe.org/2009/outreach-is-undead.

Hawk, Thomas. n.d. "Social Return on Investment." NEF—New Economics Foundation. www.neweconomics.org/projects/social-return-investment.

Jeffries, Stuart. 2010. "The Battle of Britain's Libraries." *The Guardian G2*, March 8, 17.

Juntumaa, Jouni. 2011. "The Future of Reference Service in Public Libraries." *Refer* 27, no. 2/3: 7–9.

Miller, Rebecca. 2012. "Data-Driven Libraries: Moving from Outputs to Outcomes." *Library Journal* 136, no. 21: 34.

Parliament of Australia, House of Representatives Standing Committee on Education and Employment. 2011. *Inquiry into School Libraries and Teacher Librarians in Australian Schools*. Canberra: Commonwealth of Australia.

Pew Internet and American Life Project. 2012. *The Rise of E-reading*. Washington, DC: Pew Research Center.

Purdy, Kevin. 2011. "Why In-Person Socializing Is a Mandatory To-Do Item." *Fast Company*, December 9. www.fastcompany.com/1800307/why-in-person-socializing-is-a-mandatory-to-do-item/.

Scheinfeldt, Tom. 2012. "Nobody Cares About the Library: How Digital Technology Makes the Library Invisible (and Visible) to Scholars." *Found History* (blog), February 22. www.foundhistory.org/2012/02/22/nobody-cares-about-the-library-how-digital-technology-makes-the-library-invisible-and-visible-to-scholars.

Schneider, Karen G. 2000. "The Untethered Librarian." *American Libraries* 31. www.ala.org/ala/alonline/inetlibrarian/2000columns/august2000untethered.htm.

SGS Consulting. 2011. *Dollars, Sense and Public Libraries: The Landmark Study of the Socio-economic Value of Victorian Public Libraries*. Melbourne, AU: State Library of Victoria.

Sherman, Scott. 2011. "Upheaval at the New York Library." *The Nation*, December 19. www.thenation.com/article/164881/upheaval-new-york-public-library.

Shumaker, David. 2009. "Who Let the Librarians Out? Embedded Librarianship and the Library Manager." *Reference and User Services Quarterly* 48, no. 3: 239–42, 257.

Siegal, Rene Shimada. 2012. "5 Reasons You Need to Meet in Person." *Inc.*, February 29. www.inc.com/rene-siegel/five-reasons-you-need-to-meet-in-person.html.

Sobel, Karen. 2009. "Promoting Library Reference Services to First-Year Undergraduate Students: What Works?" *Reference and User Services Quarterly* 48, no. 4: 362–71.

Stephens, Michael. 2011. "Stuck in the Past." *Library Journal* 136, no. 7: 54.

Swords, David, ed. 2011. *Patron-Driven Acquisitions: History and Best Practices*. Berlin: De Gruyter Saur.

UK Department for Culture, Media and Sport. 2011. "Next Phase of Superfast Broadband." News story, August 10. UK.gov. www.culture.gov.uk/news/news_stories/7621.aspx.

Part 3

Building New Infrastructure

Chapter 6

THE CONSTANT INNOVATOR

A New Organizational Mode of Experimentation

Megan Hodge

Libraries are slow to change. Regardless of the reasons, whether due to administrative red tape, slow publishing processes, or an actual reluctance to change, this sluggishness is no longer tenable. While caution may have served libraries well in the past, it is now a hindrance rather than an asset: the profession is unable to take advantage of new technologies and is failing to adapt to dramatic cultural shifts. Librarians are already questioning their relevance in today's society, and library patrons are questioning it as well. Libraries have become unmoored from their core mission, are unsure of which route to take and what initiatives to pursue, and have as a result lost key opportunities to influence popular culture and perception. The public has noticed.

Herbert Gerjouy stated, "Tomorrow's illiterate will not be the man who can't read; he will be the man who has not learned how to learn" (cited in Toffler 1970, 414). Similarly, libraries are in danger of becoming like a man who cannot learn because they are too slow to embrace change. Like many institutions that were created during the bricks-and-mortar era, libraries still have an "internal constituency" of people who are afraid or unwilling to acknowledge that the information landscape has changed and that libraries must change with it (Surowiecki 2010). As Jason Griffey (2011) notes, "Experiences become expectations. The experiences that our patrons have with . . . gadgets and gizmos set their expectations for their interaction with information. We need to be watching the leading edge of the bell curve of technology so that by the time these things become embedded in our patrons' lives it doesn't take us a decade to find a way to provide library services that they recognize."

Countless brick-and-mortar stores (including sometimes library rival Barnes and Noble) have discovered that convenience trumps all. "If products are available conveniently enough and cheaply enough online," write Smith and Pickett (2011, 41), "customers don't care about or need a physical store and all the accoutrements that go with it." In the early days of computers, libraries made a good-faith effort to increase convenience by transitioning from the card catalog to the online public access catalog (OPAC), but efforts have since lagged. Librarians who doubt the need for prompt action should take heed from Blockbuster's fate (Cohan 2010). In retrospect it is easy to see how Netflix won out over Blockbuster: one has a limited selection and requires a trip to the store; the other has a seemingly endless selection, unprecedented convenience, no need to leave home, and no late fees.

This does not mean, however, that all libraries should move to an online model. Regardless of the need to innovate and update core goals and missions, libraries across the country (and indeed world) serve very different demographics. Libraries could take many different physical and virtual forms. For example, in both densely and sparsely populated areas, libraries could set up bestseller book kiosks along the lines of Redbox in places where either there isn't enough space for a branch or usage wouldn't be high enough to justify a staffed building. Other libraries could take the shape of Internet cafés where people without computers or Internet access at home can complete job applications, check Facebook, and meet clients and friends, perhaps with a staff member on hand to answer questions and troubleshoot the inevitable printer problems. The mobile version of a library's website might simply serve as an "online store" where virtual reference and e-books are provided. In the many places in the United States where the public library remains the only provider of broadband Internet, libraries will more often take the shape of computer warehouses; in busy, space-limited cities, they may appear as kiosks in mass transit stations (Horrigan 2007).

A Call to Action: Taking Charge of Our Professional Destiny

Currently libraries are at the mercy of many factors outside their control: the economy, changing ideas about how to find information, and rapidly evolving technology. They are also affected by the pricing and limitations of the software—fundamental to providing basic services such as databases, integrated library systems (ILSs), and e-book delivery—that vendors provide. This is one area, at least, where libraries can regain control. It is up to librarians to take the initiative and create the software and services required to meet patron needs rather than waiting for vendors to come up with expensive solutions, especially when those solutions often fall short in providing the usability and user experience that libraries need and patrons expect. As Anthony Molaro (2012) put it, "Are the systems being designed for the user, or do we design users for the system?" Who better understands the needs of library patrons than librarians? Database interfaces, for example, are notoriously complex; many library schools offer a class in database searching for just this reason. Librarians spend countless hours teaching patrons how to use these databases, when a more logical approach would be to start from scratch and design an interface that is effective and easy to use.

In addition to continuing services that align closely with their core mission, libraries would do well to be forward-thinking and proactive instead of reactive. Immersed in a culture that values convenience above all, libraries should be looking at how to make services more convenient to patrons. For instance, they could deliver books by mail as a literary version of Netflix. They could focus on digitizing niche collections belonging to local publications and dignitaries, television and radio stations, and amateur collectors. As Alexis Madrigal (2011) stated, "Get that stuff out of the basement and put it online for free, where people can link to, remix, and use it. But don't just dump it there. Take advantage of what the web can do. Structure the work . . . so that people can improve on your collection." At the bare minimum, this could consist simply of hosting a space in the form of a local wiki or Flickr stream, such as the Library of Congress and National Library of Australia are doing. Libraries could become a place where "you go to generate ideas in the first place," innovation labs that are free and open to the public (Rundle 2011). These labs would be stocked with software and equipment (e.g., Photoshop and poster and 3D model printers) too expensive for the average person to own, and could be utilized by small businesses as well as individuals. Fayetteville (NY) Public Library's "Fab Lab" is an example of what's possible even now. Think about the possible return on investment on that service.

Overall, libraries should focus on anticipating what patrons want and work on meeting those needs immediately, rather than waiting years to see what trends will win out and then waiting again for vendors to create a service that meets those needs. This is not as outlandish as it might seem at first; there is a precedent for libraries—admittedly, large and well-staffed ones—in providing solutions for widespread problems that have been adopted at nearly every library in the country. For example, most libraries do not perform much original cataloging anymore; they use information provided by the Library of Congress. The Online Computer Library Center (OCLC) developed WorldCat .org, a one-stop shop where many library catalogs are shared and that made interlibrary loan incalculably easier.

Some libraries are already working on taking the ball out of the vendors' court. Koha and Evergreen are open source ILSs developed by libraries and extensible by other libraries, unlike other vendor-created ILSs that do not allow modification. The Kansas State Librarian is working on an alternative e-book platform, while the Darien Library in Connecticut provides a print-on-demand service for works that are self-published or in the public domain (Kelley 2001). Librarian Jim Blanton of the Chesapeake Central Library in Virginia is cofounder of ePublish or Bust, a project designed to eliminate the publisher middleman and to enable patrons to go from book concept to published work—all at their library. These are just a few examples of libraries taking control of their patrons' needs without waiting for vendor solutions.

Libraries can no longer simply provide access to information. In order to remain relevant and needed, they must do something more. As Grant (2012) points out, "We have to think about where we're adding value to that information so that when delivered to the user/member that value is recognized. Then we need to make that value part of our brand." Where do libraries add value? They help transform information into usable knowledge, as is stated explicitly in the Chesterfield County (VA) Public Library's mission statement: "Transforming data and information into usable knowledge." For all their ease of use, this is something that Google and Wikipedia cannot claim to do.

Google: A Model for Managing Innovation

Libraries continue to be underfunded and understaffed, which makes finding the time and money to create new services difficult. Many libraries have experienced layoffs, making the provision of even the bare minimum, quotidian services such as circulation and reference problematic. But in order to remain relevant and to continue providing those services that patrons will recognize as valuable now rather than 20 years ago, the time to generate, flesh out, implement, and share ideas must come from somewhere.

Some academic libraries already do this on a smaller scale by employing "emerging technologies" librarians. These librarians work with faculty and students to determine their needs, scan the literature and social media horizon for ideas, evaluate the ideas for fit within the institution, create and deliver services or tools, and make sure faculty and staff are aware of their offerings. The library of the future will look at emerging trends and technologies as well, but in a more expansive and replicable way. It is not feasible for all libraries and library systems to have an entire staff person devoted to generating big ideas; it may not even be desirable because different librarians at the same institution can have very different opinions about the same services. Frontline staff are more likely to be aware of problems in the delivery of everyday services, while technicians and administrators will be familiar with the history of such problems, attempts made to address them, and technical limitations. A superior way to innovate is by gathering a varied mix of people to think about problems and solutions in much the same way that variety enhances a species gene pool.

Getting everyone from frontline staff up to administrators on board and actively innovating is time-consuming and could disrupt the daily functions of a library. This time must be managed somehow, and indeed there is a way. Google's "20 percent time" is an inspiring model for allocating time for innovation at a sustainable level over the long term. According to Google itself, many of its best ideas, such as Gmail and AdSense, are products of 20 percent time. There are caveats, of course: the projects must be "company related" so employees can't spend a full day working on something that will be turned into their own private business. Twenty percent of a full-time employee's workweek is eight hours, or one full workday. Trying to squeeze in an hour here and an hour there to think is probably never going to happen; meetings run over, a patron has just one more question, and too many distractions clamor for attention. Having a full eight hours, on the other hand, is analogous to having parentheses on either side of one's day: a closed office door protecting one from the minutiae that pop up just from walking across the building. Another advantage to a 20 percent time program is the ability to work from home. Telecommuting is an increasingly desirable alternative work arrangement that has the additional bonus of boosting employee morale (Mariani 2000). Alternatively, one's 20 percent time could be used to meet with a group and collaborate.

Group work is an important part of how Google handles its 20 percent time. Work in grouplets (Google-speak for "teams") happens "when the thing you really want to work on is to make a broad change across the whole organization, [and] you need something new. . . . These grouplets have practically no budget, and they have no decision-making authority. What they have is a bunch of people who are committed to an idea and willing to work to convince the rest of the company to adopt it" (Mediratta and Bick 2007). These parameters—a limited or nonexistent budget and the need for a broad change—align perfectly with library needs and resources. This shift in management style from independent work and decision making to collaborative processes can improve function at the individual library level, too.

Julie Hildebrand, director of the Independence (KS) Public Library, credits such a shift for the changes that resulted in the library winning *Library Journal*'s Best Small Library in America award in 2012: "Staff are now encouraged to participate together on projects, express new ideas, and ask for help from other members of the team. Each staffer has a set of primary duties, but creativity and innovation come when they help one another with new programs and projects" (Berry 2001). As Hildebrand told *Library Journal*, "the library was dying" when she was promoted to its directorship in 2009 (Berry 2012). With financial conditions mirroring those of many libraries across the country and world, cuts needed to be made. Hildebrand and her staff of seven effected a dramatic turnaround in two years, largely through a change in management style from autocratic to participatory. Hildebrand calls this the "key" to the Independence Public Library transformation. Instead of management making all the decisions on what needed to be changed, all staff became part of the solution. By accepting the possibility of failure—a necessary corollary of encouraging innovation—and allowing staff to step outside their job-prescribed boundaries, this library's staff found the motivation and ability not only to improve their circumstances but also to win a major award in the process. Some examples of fantastic projects other librarians have come up with on their own time include Jason Griffey's LibraryBox and the State Library of Queensland's Libraryhack competition. Given the time and support, even one librarian can do something amazing.

Perhaps the most important aspect of effective national and international innovation is sharing ideas in a timely fashion. If one library comes up with an excellent new service, that library's patrons will of course be thrilled, but that is not enough. One of the library profession's greatest strengths is its willingness to share great ideas; libraries are not in competition with one another and the success of one does not injure that of another, even that of a neighbor. Of course libraries already share ideas through conference presentations and journal articles, and more informally through personal blog posts and social media, but the former methods are too slow and the latter either reach too small an audience or have a limited forum in which to expound and explain. Alternatives are needed.

The Practicalities: How All This Will Work

While it is not the place of this chapter to describe the nuts and bolts of how such a transformation will be achieved, the practicalities of how a shift in work distribution and practices will happen must be discussed to move this concept from theory to possibility.

First, buy-in at the highest levels of library administration is key. While it is important that library staff at all levels embrace the importance of transformation, workflow changes and staff redistribution simply will not happen without buy-in from the top down. Library leaders and managers must acknowledge, in an Upton Sinclair's *The Jungle*–like moment, that libraries are at a tipping point and that idea generation and service creation are critical for the profession's continued existence and relevancy. Librarians are already skilled at putting the needs of the individual and theoretical, such as privacy, over those of the corporate and tangible, so it is not such a stretch to put the needs of the library as an institution above those of the individual library from which a librarian receives a paycheck. It is vital that employees receive not only permission but also encouragement to pursue such projects.

Library administrators need not worry about their subordinates aimlessly wandering the Internet searching for ideas. Elisabeth Doucett (2010) has come up with an excellent strategy for finding, identifying, selecting, and obtaining good ideas. It may be challenging to determine which technologies will become part of library patrons' quotidian lives and which are simply fads, but predictive research, such as Gartner's *Hype Cycle for Emerging Technologies*, will help. Each year, Gartner Research publishes visual and narrative reports that "provide a graphic representation of the maturity and adoption of technologies and applications, and how they are potentially relevant to solving real business problems and exploiting new opportunities," tracking various technologies from their "trigger" to a "plateau of productivity" (Gartner Research, n.d.). These reports are published online every year, and its *Hype Cycle for Emerging Technologies* is especially useful for librarians. A similar resource is the Horizon Report (Higher Ed edition) published annually by the EDUCAUSE Learning Initiative and the New Media Consortium. Taking the conjecture out of determining what is a fad and what is the future will enable librarians to become proactive, instead of reactive, by creating solutions for problems that don't yet exist.

Next, libraries of all types must create a vision to strive toward. The profession is currently in a state of flux, a condition not unlike a midlife crisis: Who are we? What do we do? Many groups have been working on creating a vision for libraries, but unless these questions are addressed first, libraries will continue to flounder, exhausting limited resources on services that users do not expect and do not use. Cutting tangential services will free up resources necessary to implement the library's vision. As Carl Grant (2012) notes, "Our end goal should always be to become the best at providing those [core] services for our library members." Creating this vision will also save time and energy that would otherwise be spent fixing historical library problems that will not apply to the library of the future. The management philosophy known as High Performance Teams works quite well in these conditions, since it operates assuming a desire to effect "major change." As Katzenbach (1994) puts it, "What sets apart [this managerial philosophy] is the degree of commitment, particularly how deeply committed the members are to one another. . . . Such commitments extend beyond company activities and even beyond the life of the team itself." According to this philosophy, managers set an example for their employees and "think from the right" about the ideal that the institution is striving toward, where the library's current state is on the left and its vision is on the right. Contrasting the ideal with the current reality exposes the gap between existing services and practices and the institution's goals. Instead of remaining mired in fixing the myriad problems that crop up in the daily function of a library, staff can instead focus on how to make the paradigm a reality.

An additional way to think proactively instead of reactively, though this time on a more local rather than universal basis, is to hire a firm or to purchase software that will conduct in-depth customer research into the library's patron base. This sort of research is necessary to determine how librarians should focus their grouplet work time. Traditional methods of obtaining customer feedback, such as surveys, are extremely limited in their ability to reveal how patrons behave and what they need. In one well-known example, university students often clamor for their libraries to operate 24/7, but the libraries that actually accede to these requests often find that the building remains unused during the late night hours. Patrons may like the idea of a service, such as around-the-clock hours, but an expressed wish does not predict future usage. Contracting a customer research firm or purchasing customer research software "helps the library understand where patrons live, what transactions they are making, where they make those transactions, how they are behaving, what their lifestyles are. . . . It answers the questions, 'Who are we serving? Who are we not serving?' 'Who do we need to serve?' and 'Are our service strategies matching the population?'" (Miller, Fialkoff, and Kelley 2012). Obtaining this information will enable the library to connect with all the physical and virtual spaces where its patrons spend their time, so new services will be known and utilized.

Achieving transformation does not require the upending of all established workflows; on the contrary, many suggestions described here are already happening at individual libraries. For example, libraries of all types have noticed a reduction in the number of reference questions that come their way. Where once librarians handled reference by triage, patrons now rely on free, web-based services like Google and Wikipedia. Rather than reacting with dismay to a reduction in reference desk needs, librarians can look at the bright side: increased time to work on projects. Less expensive library clerks or student workers can replace librarians at the desk, as indeed they already have in many libraries, to answer ready reference questions and refer more complex ones to a librarian. Even without a pressing need for change, paying a professional librarian $20 an hour to "hang around waiting to help people read spine labels" is arguably not the best use of taxpayer or tuition dollars (Rundle 2011).

The Google grouplets model of organized innovation takes advantage of one of the most wonderful characteristics innate to our profession: to share, rather than hoard, good ideas that work. Currently, this sharing of ideas takes place informally through word of mouth, Twitter, and blogs, and formally through journal articles and conference presentations. These methods all have serious drawbacks, discussed previously, that prevent them from being utilized as media through which to share instantaneous, useful information. However, these methods are the only substantial ways in which librarians share ideas and collaborate. Even at the institutional level, how many libraries—or organizations of any type—have a reliable, accessible medium through which to disseminate success stories? On the other end of the spectrum there is the librarian "in the field," working "largely in isolation on a daily basis," encountering the same challenges as her colleagues in the library the next town or state over (Rundle 2011). Not all of these problems are worth discussing at the conference or peer-reviewed-article level, but these librarians would certainly benefit from increased collaboration with their peers. As Steve Matthews (2011) points out, "Doesn't sharing experiences with colleagues equate to professional development? Who doesn't need professional development?"

What is needed is a centralized conduit through which information can pass so librarians need not read dozens or hundreds of different information feeds. This conduit could be a centralized repository, a Library of Congress of good ideas. Publishing all submissions would quickly result in information overload, so the conduit's moderators could publish the best of the best and store honorable mentions in a searchable digital warehouse. Ideally, this conduit would be able to share information quickly and inexpensively and organize ideas by topic: readers' advisory, collection management, and so on. The Netherlands-based Internet TV series *This Week in Libraries*, which "features global library news and interviews with individuals involved in library innovation," is already doing something along these lines ("Global Reach" 2010). Such a conduit, whether an Internet television series, a podcast, or a news feed blog with quick links, could become a Channel One for librarians, where watching the latest installment at the start of every workday or week could be obligatory, as it is for many of today's schoolchildren.

Conclusion

Bogged down by bureaucracy and professional caution, libraries in general move too slowly to embrace new technologies and cultural shifts. The current challenge to librarians is to take the initiative and create the software and services required to meet patron needs rather than waiting for vendors to come up with solutions and then paying exorbitant amounts of money for those solutions. However, libraries continue to be underfunded and understaffed, making finding the time and money to create these services difficult. In the library of the future, there will be acknowledgment at the highest levels of library administration that idea generation and service creation are vital for the continued existence and relevance of the individual library and the profession at large. All staff will be expected and encouraged to use one workday, or roughly 20 percent of their time, to work on forward-thinking projects each week.

Librarians will return from these weekly grouplet work sessions rejuvenated and excited about ideas that can be implemented in their libraries. On these workdays, library staff will either teleconference with their colleagues around the nation and world or meet face-to-face to collaborate. There will be official clearinghouses (adaptations of sites like Dolores' List of CFPs and ALA Connect's Opportunities Exchange) where project ideas will be posted when collaborators are needed, and depending on the size and prestige of the project, appointment to some of these projects will be competitive. Library staff will also be able to develop grouplets organically through informal means.

Once projects are ready for beta testing, project librarians' home institutions will have first dibs on trying them. Projects that require additional libraries or different library types will also be posted to the central clearinghouse, with applications as necessary for the more prestigious projects. Completed projects would then be published to the global library news outlet.

The benefits of adopting a Google grouplets model of innovation are many. Libraries will no longer be bogged down by bureaucracy and professional caution, unable to adapt quickly to new technologies and cultural shifts. They will be able to take the initiative and create the software and services they need. Libraries continue to be underfunded and understaffed, but by distributing the time for innovation among all current staff members, they will have more time and money to create new services and hire new staff. Staff will enjoy improved morale because they will grow beyond their quotidian duties and become invested in the big picture of the profession. As Mediratta notes, "It sounds obvious, but people work better when they're involved in something they're passionate about" (Mediratta and Bick 2007). Most importantly, the profession will be nimbler and more dynamic, more effectively staying ahead of trends and providing services that that not only meet the needs of patrons but also amaze them.

References

Berry, John N., III. 2012. "Best Small Library in America 2012: The Independence Public Library, KS." *Library Journal* (January 31). http://lj.libraryjournal.com/2012/01/managing-libraries/best-small-library-in-america-2012-the-independence-public-library-ks.

Cohan, Peter. 2010. "Why Blockbuster Went Bust While Netflix Flourished." *Daily Finance* (blog), September 23. www.dailyfinance.com/2010/09/23/why-blockbuster-went-bust-while-netflix-flourished.

Doucett, Elisabeth. 2010. *What They Don't Teach You in Library School*. Chicago: American Library Association.

Gartner Research. n.d. "Hype Cycles." Research Methodologies. www.gartner.com/technology/research/methodologies/hype-cycle.jsp.

"Global Reach." 2010. *American Libraries* (May): 17.

Grant, Carl. 2012. "Are Librarians Choosing to Disappear from the Information and Knowledge Delivery Process?" *Thoughts from Carl Grant* (blog). Tuesday, February 28. http://thoughts.care-affiliates.com/2012/02/are-librarians-choosing-to-disappear.html.

Griffey, Jason. 2011. "CES: The Librarian's Takeaway." *American Libraries, US and World News* (blog), Monday, February 28 (16:47). http://americanlibrariesmagazine.org/news/02282011/ces-librarian-s-takeaway.

Horrigan, John. 2007. "Closing the Broadband Divide." Pew Internet and American Life Project. www.pewinternet.org/Reports/2007/Closing-the-Broadband-Divide/Why-it-will-Be-Hard-to-Close-the-Broadband-Divide.aspx.

"How the World Sees Us." 2010. *American Libraries* (May): 22.

Katzenbach, Jon R., and Douglas K. Smith. 1994. *The Wisdom of Teams: Creating the High-Performance Organization*. New York: HarperBusiness.

Kelley, Michael. 2011. "Kansas State Librarian Can Transfer Thousands of Titles from OverDrive to 3M at No Charge." *Library Journal* (October 10). www.libraryjournal.com/lj/newsletters/newsletterbucketljxpress/892348-441/kansas_state_librarian_can_transfer.html.csp.

Madrigal, Alexis. 2011. "What Big Media Can Learn from the New York Public Library." *The Atlantic*, June 20. www.theatlantic.com/technology/archive/2011/06/what-big-media-can-learn-from-the-new-york-public-library/240565/1/%3Futm_content%3Dianlibrarian%2540live.co.uk.

Mariani, Matthew. 2000. "Telecommuters." *Occupational Outlook Quarterly* (Fall). www.bls.gov/opub/ooq/2000/fall/art02.pdf.

Matthews, Steve. 2011. "Why Don't Librarians Collaborate More?" *21st Century Library Blog*, December 14. http://21stcenturylibrary.com/2011/12/14/why-dont-librarians-collaborate-more.

Mediratta, Bharat, as told to Julie Bick. 2007. "The Google Way: Give Engineers Room." *New York Times*, October 21. www.nytimes.com/2007/10/21/jobs/21pre .html?_r=1.

Miller, Rebecca, Francine Fialkoff, and Michael Kelley. 2012. "Data-Driven Libraries: Moving from Outputs to Outcomes." *Library Journal* (January 26). http://lj.library journal.com/2012/01/managing-libraries/data-driven-libraries-moving-from -outputs-to-outcomes.

Molaro, Anthony. 2012. "IA Greatest Hits: The Apple Way for Libraries (A Manifesto?)." *The Information Activist Librarian* (blog), April 12. http://informationactivist.com/ 2012/04/12/ia-greatest-hits-the-apple-way-for-libraries-a-manifesto.

Rundle, Hugh. 2012. "Libraries as Software—Dematerialising, Platforms and Return- ing to First Principles." *It's Not about the Books* (blog), April 4. http://hughrundle .net/2012/04/04/libraries-as-software-dematerialising-platforms-and-returning -to-first-principles.

Smith, Steven E., and Carmelita Pickett. 2011. "Avoiding the Path to Obsolescence." *American Libraries* (September/October).

Stephens, Michael. 2012. "Learning Everywhere." *Office Hours, a Library Journal blog*, April 25. http://lj.libraryjournal.com/2012/04/opinion/michael-stephens/learning -everywhere-office-hours.

Surowiecki, James. 2010. "The Next Level." *The New Yorker*, October 18. www.new yorker.com/talk/financial/2010/10/18/101018ta_talk_surowiecki.

Toffler, A. 1970. *Future Shock*. New York: Bantam.

Chapter 7

THE FUTURE OF FUNDING

A Proposal for a National Library Card

John Chrastka

It does not matter what the public library looks like, offers, circulates, collects, or programs in 2025. It only matters that it is funded.

The history of library funding shows a movement from a private, subscription-based model to cooperative, taxpayer-supported institutions with a defined service area (Akst 2012). Each of these models provides funders with a library card to access collections and services. In the earliest examples, the library card given to private subscribers offered exclusive access to a limited collection. In the association or club funding model, the organizers issued library cards more widely, intending some public benefit from their largesse. As the local levy began to support wide-scale public access, the library card took on its current role as a gateway to ever-larger collections and a better-educated library workforce.

The library as we know it today rests on the triumph of the early twentieth-century progressive movement and the notion that the government should play a role in people's lives and livelihoods (Cyphers 2002). Institutions like public schools, health departments, public safety, parks, public transportation, and libraries sprang from the belief that cooperatively funding services through progressive taxation policy could improve society as a whole. In fact, state and federal support for library cooperation and innovation is a relatively recent development in the 300-year history of libraries in the United States (Holley 1983). Each of the institutions mentioned has provided the populace with a measure of support by pooling resources for the common good. Public schooling from preschool through college serves as the cornerstone of an educated and capable workforce. Health and public safety institutions provide potable water and fight fires. Parks and public transportation systems provide recreation and ease access around crowded cities and remote locations alike. Libraries historically have acted as centers for learning, enjoyment, civic engagement, and personal enrichment (Kranich 2001).

Local tax support for public institutions is also a legacy of the Progressive Era (Jansson 2012). But as an artifact from those times, the definition of what is local has been outpaced by the mobility of the populace (Kunstler 1994). Developed in a period before widespread car ownership and significantly different patterns of service access, using locally levied taxes for exclusively local goals was a reasonable community behavior. As personal transportation has begun to obviate distance, it has become common for people to travel beyond their own local taxing districts to access services like parks and libraries. The magnet and charter school movements have allowed parents a degree of flexibility beyond specific school borders when making education choices. In the larger social picture, the rise of so-called megachurches demonstrates that people are no longer tied to parochial boundaries (Bird and Scott 2011), while destination shopping malls and big box stores have moved retail spending to centralized locations (Kunstler 1998). For certain library users, it is inevitable that changes to format and online content delivery will dramatically impact their core reasons to visit the physical library.

As with other institutions from the Progressive Era, funding for libraries is to a large extent prescribed by relatively small geographies that overlap with taxing authorities' boundaries. Local revenue models vary across the country, with some jurisdictions levying against property, some against sales tax, and others as a component of fees or use taxes. Those few states that have a library line item in the annual budget do not constitutionally enshrine libraries as a guarantee to citizens in the same way they do public education, leaving libraries exposed to vagaries of the budgeting process. In every instance, federal and state support is formulaically allocated through grants or on a per-capita basis. While programs from the Institute for Museum and Library Services (IMLS) and the US Department of Education are essential conduits for federal funds, neither formula can sustain our institutions, nor are they adequate to fill in gaps when the primary funding source is bound by population or local economies.

When nonlocal sources of funding are limited to a few dollars per head, the effectiveness of each library card is limited by a geography that is tied to local taxes. As we have seen during the recent recession, without a diverse funding stream from multiple sources (Hussey and Velasquez 2011), library funding is always in peril to local and regional forces (Lance, Hofschire, and Daisey 2011).

Realign by 2025

By 2025, the library community needs to address the current ad hoc system of local, state, and federal funding to create a new, sustaining method for funding library services beyond local taxing districts and limited state and federal programs. A National Library Card, embodying the notion of universal access to the universe of information in libraries, should be the rallying point for this campaign. The techniques necessary to accomplish such a significant realignment in funding sources are varied and extend across governmental, corporate, and private sectors. For instance, new emphasis must be placed on improving the amount and nature of governmental support to libraries at all levels. A new approach to charitable deductions for libraries in the tax code in which libraries are earmarked as a special class of grantee will radically alter the sustainability of libraries for the public good.

Of course, significant political hurdles challenge the potential of this realignment. Long-standing precedents in tax policy and deep-seated perceptions about local control need to be analyzed and addressed with transparency and candor. The library community itself must radically engage the discussion about the role libraries play in civil society, and clearly demonstrate how they positively affect public education and the economy. Creating a National Library Card for 2025 will signal a new movement for libraries in this country and reignite within the public the promise of access to information, entertainment, and personal enrichment in libraries. Funding the goals of a national card, and therefore the libraries that serve those goals, requires innovative thinking and bold policy choices.

Four techniques should be advanced with policymakers to build this new funding model. First, establishing a national card and a federal mechanism to fund its goals is essential. The next two techniques look back to the Progressive Era roots of the modern library for inspiration by using the tax code to effectively move this social good forward. Explicitly placing libraries in the tax code will encourage new and significant corporate, foundation, and private support specifically for libraries. Further, using Social Impact Bonds as a way to finance construction, infrastructure improvements, collections, programs, and services will dramatically increase capital resources for libraries beyond local jurisdictions. Finally, the creation of a National Trust for Libraries will encourage private and corporate donors to give to libraries as an institution.

Establishing a National Library Card

A National Library Card is aspirational: it ensures that everyone has access to information in all its forms and across all delivery channels regardless of geography. At its simplest, a national card will serve to enfranchise all citizens with access to a library, both as a place and as a resource. The card will guarantee access to programs, collections, and services, whether delivered in person or online. Specific goals for the national card will emerge as we move ahead in discovering, designing, and implementing solutions to new problems but should be based in the core, historic, and humane services offered by modern libraries. This proposal for a National Library Card and a new formula for increased funding assume continuing evolution and adaption by libraries to cultural and technological shifts.

Changing the funding formula from primarily local sources to a hybrid that includes significant federal allocations along with corporate and private contributions will require a generational commitment on the part of the library community. This is not a proposal to simply increase federal support to libraries in a particular budget year. While it is extremely important to improve federal funding, relying solely on the budget process means that in every budget year the library community is either gifted with incremental positive changes in revenue or subjected to cuts that are at best proportional and at worst capricious and damaging. Without an expansion of funding, our hopes and dreams for libraries in 2025 will be diminished or curtailed. Without new funding, the ideals of a National Library Card and what it represents for access and individual freedoms will simply not be realized.

Through 2025, the library community should continue to advocate for IMLS and legislative initiatives that increase funding through the institute. As we approach 2025, we must also challenge policymakers to create a new National Trust for Libraries that will act as a repository for corporate and private contributions, discussed following, and serve as a channel for directly supporting the national card's goals.

While the format of library collections will continue to evolve through 2025 with more electronic delivery of books, movies, and media, the core assumption of this chapter is that the provision of access to some form of printed material will continue for the foreseeable future. This means that the library will continue to be a place to select and acquire media and will function as a destination in place as well as online. A national card needs to include immediate access to collections, services, and programs regardless of geography or jurisdiction. In a true national system, individuals should be able to go into any library and get the item of their choice. If they obtain a physical copy, the same individuals should be able to return the item at any other library or by mail, and the library would be secure in knowing that the material would be returned to its rightful home. The infrastructure requirements to accomplish such a successful cooperation are within reach, as many libraries have already established regional systems that accomplish the same ends. The logistics of expanding such cooperation and moving items around the country are well established in the private sector.

A key question is one of ownership of the items or licenses being circulated. It is not likely that by 2025 the jurisdictional issues of local ownership of library materials will be resolved. The time frame is too short and the political environment too fraught with provincial concerns about local control and local spending. The national card needs a public-private partnership in order to succeed. In fact, several partnerships for the public good are necessary to see the goals of the card come into existence. When considering circulating an item or providing digital access to an individual who is not a local taxpayer at that library, the questions of replacement and accountability need to be addressed. If a mechanism were available to secure the value of that item for the originating library, concerns about the reliable return of that item would be obviated. Several sponsors for this service exist, most notably the major credit and debit card issuers.

While stopping short of suggesting that Visa or MasterCard become the de facto National Library Card, the elegance of enfranchising access outside of one's own local jurisdiction based on a different kind of hold should be considered. The opportunity for one of the major card issuers to bid on and support the goals of the National Library Card for a multiyear period would provide notable returns to the company while allowing patrons immediate access to collections all across the country. Of course, the winning bidder would waive transaction costs for libraries and provide processing systems.

For the system to succeed, the item must be returned. The library community can again look to a public-private partnership for underwriting and support. Logistics companies like FedEx and UPS could provide the labeling and packaging at checkout, which would make transportation quick, safe, and effective for the returns. Likewise, the winning corporate bidder would absorb the costs of moving materials between libraries as a condition of their named sponsorship of America's libraries. The library community can learn from the early successes of Netflix in moving flat media and Hewlett-Packard in moving fragile but expensive ink cartridges around the country.

While inspiration for the national card comes from the many regional or state models, an aspiration for finding an overarching and sustaining funding source for the card is rooted in the fact that these initiatives currently rise and fall depending on budgetary challenges and the vision of library leadership in

the service area. If libraries are limited by the notion that a library, both physical and virtual, can only provide access to what can be stored in the building
or afforded online, then a robustly funded and properly supported national
card expands their possibilities. If every library has the same access to materials and information, then the library itself is freed of limitations in the eyes of
the public and empowered to more effectively support its mission.

Embedding Libraries in the Tax Code

The tax code is commonly used in this country to encourage corporations to
behave in specific ways. A relevant example is a progressive tax policy designed to encourage businesses to hire veterans by providing tax breaks and
credits to businesses that hire and retain those workers. In designating veterans as a preferred class of job candidate, the federal government encourages
the hiring of highly trained and qualified individuals who may not have a traditional résumé. Individual families and specific businesses benefit from this
policy through gainful employment and payroll tax offsets. The library community should be inspired by this and look to the tax code as a way to encourage new and significant funding from corporations.

Every sector of the US economy benefits from the impact that libraries have
on education, the local economy, and business development. By 2025, the library community must challenge policymakers to designate libraries as a preferred recipient for charitable contributions by large corporations and small
business alike, and to return a more significant tax benefit for this charitable
support than is currently offered. Donations can be made directly to a particular library or can be channeled to the trust established to support the national
card, perhaps through IMLS. In either case, corporate donations should be encouraged and rewarded through proportionally larger tax offsets and credits.

As a related issue, corporate and private foundations regularly make a
significant mistake when issuing grant applications by omitting libraries as
a class of eligible institutions (Moore 2005). All libraries in this country should
be explicitly designated as 501(c)(3) charitable institutions in the tax code,
and therefore automatically eligible for donations. This simple technique will
end the unintentional and unfortunate omission of libraries from many grant
programs. While this change will not significantly affect the nature of corporate grant programs, dispelling confusion about every library's status as an educational charity in addition to continuing as a unit of government will open
libraries up to new sources of transitional or programmatic support.

The tax code can be put to further good work by making donations to libraries a shelter for estate and inheritance taxes. By 2025, the first significant

wave of baby boomer estates will be struggling with issues of inheritance tax. For every dollar contributed to libraries by a will, bequest, or estate transfer, a proportionally larger offset should be afforded to heirs and assignees on the remainder of the estate. Designating libraries as a special class for personal legacy donations not only will encourage individuals to consider our institutions during estate planning but will also enable financial planners, insurance underwriters, and the legal community to leverage library giving on behalf of their clients. Again, funds can be either designated to a particular library or given to the trust supporting the national card. In either instance, doubling or tripling the relative value of that donation will dramatically increase the frequency of donating and the amount given. Aligning this support with the ongoing impact that well-funded libraries provide generationally will resonate with intentional givers and strategy-minded planners alike.

Social Impact Bonds and Libraries

Several countries are currently experimenting with new ways to leverage private and corporate financing in the bond market toward a public good. Social Impact Bonds (SIBs) are conceived as a method of financing public debt by tying returns and interest rates to the measurable success of a public program for societal good. A public body develops a program or service, and debt in the form of a bond is issued to underwrite expenses. Where SIBs differ from ordinary debt obligations is that the public body not only seeks funding from capital markets but also agrees to pay a higher rate of return upon the measured, benchmarked, and successful completion of the project goals. The bond is floated to private and philanthropic investors who are looking for a higher rate of return and a unique alignment with social outcomes through their investments.

Libraries are uniquely positioned to utilize these new financial instruments when presenting bond offerings for buildings, collections, and infrastructure improvements as well as programs and services. In many cases, underwriters only look at the amount of taxing, levies, or millages a library jurisdiction has authorized when offering rates of return. The fact that libraries exist for the public good and have measurable educational and civic impact is now incidental but could become central to the success of library bonding if the offering is made as an SIB.

A Public-Private Trust for Libraries

Libraries need a new Dale Carnegie willing to fund construction or rebuilding of libraries' physical spaces for future generations of users, or the next Bill

Gates willing to fund the technological backbone of libraries as we move into a completely on-demand entertainment environment. However, it may be another 100 years before the industry again sees another flood of philanthropic money to rival those individual donors. Libraries cannot wait for the next windfall; instead, they would be wise to take advantage of a current trend in government to create public-private partnerships focused on local and regional infrastructure improvements.

As discussed earlier, a number of specific and limited changes to the tax code could make libraries a first choice for charitable giving from both personal and corporate sources. But donations limited to individual libraries will only reinforce existing disparities based on the demographics of donors and their communities. For the national card to succeed it will be necessary to create a mechanism for aggregating donations and encouraging new levels of support by the corporate community and individual philanthropists.

A National Trust for Libraries should be established as a public-private corporation to provide a place for private and corporate donors to give to the common cause and allow spending to be matched by federal and state commitments to the system. Corporate, foundation, and private partners will be encouraged to donate directly to the trust, secure in the knowledge that their donations will be matched by public funds—either taxes or bonds—and incentivized by offsets and tax breaks. This model is designed to focus spending on specific types of projects for the common good, such as bridges, green buildings, or telecommunications.

At its inception, the National Trust for Libraries should be focused on realizing the goals of the national card through infrastructure improvements. If we acknowledge that by 2025 library buildings and spaces will be used in significantly different ways than they are today, a public-private trust to modify, expand, or retrofit spaces would be put to good use. Infrastructure improvements will continue to be made to Internet connectivity and speed. The trust should be inaugurated with the expressed goal of funding public access to databases and other paywall-protected sources of information. Funding the National Library Card through the National Trust for Libraries would ensure that library buildings and their Internet backbone would be adequate to 2025 service tasks, while guaranteeing that collections remain robust enough to serve the public.

Reengaging First Use

This essay began with the premise that the progressive movement created a social climate where libraries were able to grow and meet the civic, educational, and entertainment needs of the public for the common good. But another Progressive Era ideal, the right of first use, forms the bedrock on which every library stands today. Many significant threats to this right need to be addressed by the library community not only as a constituency with a direct, institutional stake in the outcome but also as agents or representatives for the public-at-large on whose behalf we purchase and lend materials and provide access. It is the erosion of the right of any buyer—an individual, a wholesaler, or a library—to retain an item, resell it, lend it, or even destroy it that will be a battleground through 2025 and beyond.

While there are significant legal, regulatory, and logistical issues brought up in this essay, the most significant challenge for libraries will be as a major player in issues around electronic content and licensing. If the interests of the content creators and owners continue to be paramount and trump both the rights of buyers to use their purchases and benefits to the common good from those creations, all the other ideas for libraries floated previously will be moot.

It does not matter, in the end, what the licensing looks like for libraries. Only that libraries exist as, at the very least, an exception to the paywall, a way around a shrink-wrap agreement and back into the additive role that access to information plays both in the life of the individual and for the good of our society. Because on January 2, 2025, when everyone will be in line to obtain their National Library Card, we as an industry and a profession must be able to say, "Look what we have for you. It is just what you need, and it is free. Enjoy."

References

Akst, Daniel. 2012. "Today's Public Libraries: Public Places of Excellence, Education and Innovation." *Carnegie Reporter* 6, no. 4. http://carnegie.org/publications/carnegie-reporter/single/view/article/item/309.

Bird, Warren, and Scott Thumma. 2011. "A New Decade of Megachurches." Hartford Institute for Religion Research. www.hartfordinstitute.org/megachurch/megachurch-2011-summary-report.htm.

Cyphers, Christopher J. 2002. *The National Civic Federation and the Making of a New Liberalism*. Westport, CT: Greenwood Publishing.

Holley, Edward G., and Robert F. Schremser. 1983. *Library Services and Construction Act: An Historical Overview from the Viewpoint of Major Participants*. Greenwich, CT: JAI Press.

Hussey, Lisa K., and Diane L. Velasquez. 2011. "Forced Advocacy: How Communities Respond to Library Budget Cuts." In *Advances in Librarianship 34: Librarianship in Times of Crisis*, edited by Anne Woodsworth, 59–93. Bingley, UK: Emerald Publishing Group.

Jansson, Bruce. 2012. *The Reluctant Welfare State*. Belmont, CA: Brooks/Cole Cengage Learning.

Kranich, Nancy, ed. 2001. *Libraries and Democracy*. Chicago: American Library Association.

Kunstler, James Howard. 1994. *The Geography of Nowhere*. New York: Touchstone.

———. 1998. *Home from Nowhere*. New York: Touchstone.

Lance, Keith Curry, Linda Hofschire, and Jamie Daisey. 2011. "The Impact of the Recession on Public Library Use in Colorado." *Closer Look Report*. Denver: Colorado State Library, Library Research Service.

Moore, Mary Y. 2005. *The Successful Library Trustee Handbook*. Chicago: American Library Association.

Part 4

———————

The Global Future

Chapter 8

INTERNATIONAL SCHOOL LIBRARIES
Current Status and Future Vision

Lesley Farmer

Envisioning the future of libraries in the United States is admittedly challenging, and attempting to anticipate a future for international school libraries, with all their cultural and geographical variations, is doubly so. To begin with, libraries around the world differ dramatically in terms of the resources, services, and programs they currently provide (UNESCO 2003). Some are graced with distinguished collections and unlimited Internet access in attractive settings, while others languish with a handful of outdated materials beyond the reach of electricity. In some cases, school librarians have a self-contained classroom, while in others the classroom teacher does all the "library skills" instruction. Some countries mandate that every school must have a school library and a qualified school librarian, while others make no legislative mention of libraries at all. The training required for librarians also varies widely, from no training to an undergraduate or graduate degree. While the International Federation of Library Associations and UNESCO have developed a manifesto (1999) and guidelines (2002) for school libraries, the actualization of these statements differs greatly across and within countries.

With such intense variability, how does one attempt to envision a future for international libraries? In this chapter I will describe three nations, Nepal, Honduras, and Brazil, whose school libraries I have come to know through studies that were supported by Fulbright and the International Association of School Librarianship (IASL). By identifying their common needs and challenges, I will then outline a future vision for the International Library 2025.

Case Study One: Nepal

The Nepalese do not place much value on reading, although there is a great interest in the arts, religion, ethnicities, and nationalism. As the IASL vice president for association relations, I took the opportunity to visit school librarians and local leaders Sharada Siwakoti and Mahadev Parvate in Kathmandu. They view collection development and librarian preparation as the two primary challenges for school librarianship in their country.

Collection Development

Several factors constrain collection development in Nepal, including limited publishing, unstable or unavailable technology, lack of funds, lack of professional training, and lack of support. School libraries are vocal in soliciting book donations despite the fact that gifted items are not always relevant to the school community. They actively seek to obtain Internet-connected computers to increase the school community's access to online materials, although the country has frequent electricity interruptions and scheduled blackout times. Some libraries include materials created by the local community; in one school library, handmade oversized cloth "poster" books explain proper hygiene practices, which is a significant issue in Kathmandu. Indeed, the meager availability of Nepalese children's books has led at least one school librarian to pursue a local self-publishing effort as a potentially more effective and authentic strategy to increase the collection of reliable, relevant resources. In this effort, students would interview local experts such as business people and artisans and write up their reports to be added to the library collection, thus leveraging youth's cultural interests and needs. National and international businesses located in-country could also be encouraged to donate copies of their public documents such as travel brochures as a way to provide useful information and build partnerships with schools.

Librarian Training

One library school exists in Nepal but does not offer any courses targeted to school librarianship. Instead, the national government has delegated school librarianship training authority to the Nepalese Association of School Librarians (NASL), which provides courses for prospective and current school librarians. The NASL identified a need to create standards for school libraries and librarians and in 2008 held a national school library summit, gathering stakeholders to discuss the school library's significance in Nepal's education. The group is starting a "No Library No School" campaign and hopes to add a mandate requiring every school to have both a library and a professional teacher-librarian to the revised Nepalese constitution.

Outlook

If current conditions continue, Nepal's school librarians have the bleakest future of the three countries described in this chapter. Nepal is one of the poorest countries in the world, and current economics have curtailed tourism and international investments, both of which sustain Nepal. In terms of education, Nepalese school librarians banked on school libraries being incorporated into the new constitution, but the deadline for developing that document has been extended with little result. The country has witnessed political change, becoming a fragile democracy, and struggles with Maoist party leaders and mainland China's territorial interests. Regardless, school librarians would do well to continue their political advocacy efforts, which have seen some success. Because the government delegated school librarianship preparation to one of their two national school library associations, the group may be able to continue training efforts "under the radar." However, both school librarian associations will need succession plans to make the groups viable in the future.

Technology trends may improve this picture. Currently, energy sources are somewhat unstable, but if the country can support a major hydropower initiative, a national utility infrastructure could better support telecommunications. The rise in mobile technologies and low-cost computers further facilitates access to digital resources. As social media are harnessed in Nepal, the school community can leverage its ideas for self-publishing and work together with local entities to produce relevant digital resources that can be organized centrally by the school librarians. Furthermore, remote villages that are currently underserved will have increased access to school librarianship training online, whether in-country or accessed via international library associations.

Overall, Nepal's school library future largely depends on the rest of the world to improve the economic picture, to keep China from overcoming the country, to sustain and improve technology telecommunications access, and to create digital resources and professional training that Nepalese school librarians can access and use.

Case Study Two: Honduras

Honduras has almost eight million people. About 80 percent are functionally literate, with the upcoming generation about 90 percent literate. Nevertheless, only 60 percent of children graduate from grade school, and the reading culture is not very prevalent here. While school libraries exist, mainly in urban settings, they are sometimes just small warehouses of print materials. Many include computers with Internet access, as infrastructure is a high priority for the Honduran government. Private school libraries are more likely to have current materials in different formats as well as professional school librarians. The Tegucigalpa Bi-National Center library, for instance, sponsors field trips from local public schools to see its library and get training.

Librarian Training

The Ministry of Culture's Institute of Books and Documents provides short-term training for school librarians, who are usually teachers. In addition, the Regional Center for Book Development in Latin America, a branch of UNESCO, works with the Honduran Ministry of Culture, Arts, and Sports to advance the development and integration of the region through literacy projects. The center works with public and school libraries in the region, supporting them through training and research in the social and economic value of reading and how libraries can advance their own communities.

The US embassy in Honduras, which is held in high regard by librarians in Central America, has supported library education for years. The associated Information Resource Center (IRC) provides ad hoc training for librarians, including school librarians, on a variety of topics that includes the use of IRC resources. The IRC is pilot-testing an online web portal of free resources, which is very attractive to Honduran librarians. They are hungry for databases but usually have little funding for subscriptions. The portal is provided in Spanish and English; the Spanish version is receiving high praise, while the English version will help users become bilingual. The embassy also assists binational centers that provide English instruction.

The main driving force for developing the profession, including school libraries, is the Association of Honduran Librarians and Information Professionals (ABIDH). This national librarians association started six years ago and provides valuable local training for its members throughout the year. The ABIDH annual national conference draws librarian practitioners and educators from around the country and other Latin American countries. Both entry-level and advanced training are offered. The ABIDH has worked closely with the National Pedagogical University Francisco Morazan (2011) to develop a master's degree program in library and information science, which is the first time that such an academic program has been considered in Honduras.

Technology

As noted in the National Pedagogical University Francisco Morazan report, *Plan of Graduate Studies in Library Science Master's Degree* (2011), even those

Hondurans who are not very literate or computer-savvy see the potential of mobile technology and use it to get information. Honduran librarians eagerly use some technologies such as databases and Facebook but are less knowledgeable about virtual libraries and the use of mobile technologies. For instance, they have not yet leveraged mobile database formats, which would be very attractive due to the popularity of mobile phones in the country. While bandwidth is a challenge that needs to be addressed, low bandwidth solutions such as instant messaging, SMS, pod/vidcasts, and web-based tutorials could be explored and leveraged. The Honduran government, in collaboration with librarians, could provide public information such as health and other public services via mobile technology, especially for preliterate and functionally literate people who depend on oral communication.

Outlook

According to the National Pedagogical University Francisco Morazan report (2011), Honduran education and school libraries have potential, but it is a long way to go to reach that potential. During the last several years Honduras underwent difficult political and economic times. The situation appears to have stabilized now, and Honduras has reentered the Organization of American States. The government has high hopes for the ability of improved telecommunications and supporting infrastructure to advance initiatives, including access to information. Nevertheless, corruption and retaliation among political parties still exists, and the country is dealing with the lingering impacts of national disasters and energy constraints.

Honduran libraries have much potential if they equip themselves to leverage emerging technologies and proactively insert themselves into lifelong educational opportunities. The best scenario in Honduras would build on the continued success of the ABIDH. If this organization can bring different kinds of libraries together to create a national repository of information resources, it can optimize face-to-face and virtual access to information. However, they will need to work successfully with different government agencies to financially support these efforts. The US embassy would ideally play a key role in the initiative, but the United States is likely to reduce international offices in the future. While online services and resources may continue to be provided, this important source of support may disappear as a physical place. The loss of such face-to-face contact, which is so important in Honduran culture, would stifle progress.

Strong in-country leadership, reinforced by resource-rich international partnerships, is critical to supporting Honduran education and libraries. Only then will school libraries have the necessary material and digital resources for school communities, and only then will they have the technological and instructional training to ensure physical and intellectual access to the information needed by Hondurans. Both public and school librarians need to help youth gain the habit of reading and learn how to be independent learners, and to teach them appropriate and proactive uses of technology (American Association of School Librarians 2009). This foundation can then accelerate and deepen university and informal education.

Case Study Three: Brazil

Brazil's youth population is booming. Teens enjoy the Internet, video, and shopping more than reading. A growing number are involved in drugs, gangs, and risky sexual behavior. Many youths are interested in technology and in the Internet specifically, but few have connectivity, particularly in rural areas. Poor rural people are coming into the cities, thinking that they will get jobs and money, yet they find it very difficult to find work without literacy skills because there is great competition for manual jobs.

Most people do not have the library "habit." It is not a significant part of their culture, which is oral based, so librarians try very hard to make libraries welcoming and relevant. Librarians are increasingly doing outreach work, such as publicizing their resources and services in public areas and offering events and contests to attract youth to come to the library and become regular users. Programs that focus on creative expression such as origami clubs, folkloric dance, and jazz music are particularly popular. Even when library systems are centrally administered, however, youth projects tend to be locally driven and isolated. There is a need to coordinate program efforts within and across systems and agencies to increase impact. Several libraries have begun offering Internet access, although rural libraries sometimes lack even electricity. There is a strong need for information literacy instruction.

School libraries and librarians reflect Brazil's political and educational realities. Youths are required to attend only eight years of formal schooling, and 80 percent attend private schools, so public education is uneven at best. Most public schools operate in shifts because of overcrowding and lack of financial support. With their independent funding, private schools typically have better stocked and better staffed libraries. There is a wide spectrum of quality in terms of collections, selection, acquisitions, staff, facilities, access, instruction, curriculum, and collaboration—from poor, uncataloged donation-based collections with little access to rich, grade-specific libraries with expansive collections, strong educational activities, and well-trained teacher librarians. While some school librarians provide high-quality programs, many do not have proper training. All too often "burned out" or retired teachers are assigned to the school library. Academic library preparation dedicates little coursework targeted especially for school librarianship. Most librarianship programs are undergraduate degree programs that focus on basic operations.

In the past five years several initiatives have furthered school libraries. One national program in schools is focusing on improving literacy through resources, information literacy, and staff training. The Federal Council of Librarianship and its regional and state councils are government entities administered by elected librarians to monitor the librarianship profession. These councils launched the School Library Project to create support for school libraries. Representatives met with decision makers to explore the possibility of mandating school libraries in every school, with the resultant Law 12244 passed in 2010 to that effect, with the goal to be achieved by 2020 (Campello 2009).

Librarian Training

The University of Sao Paulo has a model school where preservice teachers can observe good practices, including a school library program. On a practical level, the Rede Escolar des Bibliotecas Interactivas is a university-based initiative that has created more than 80 school libraries that foster information literacy, reading, and culture. More systematically, the School Library Research Group, based at the School of Information Science at the Federal University of Minas Gerais, is focusing on school library research and education. In addition, the Federal Council of Librarianship holds regular workshops and conferences for school librarians, sometimes partnering with other agencies and professional associations such as the International Federation of Library Associations and Institutions, the International Association for School Librarianship, the United States International Resource Centers, and the national bilingual centers. The council also links up with the biannual meeting of the Brazilian National Federation of Librarians to lower costs and bring in more attendees. In addition, these professional library associations disseminate professional publications to their members and publicly recognize outstanding practitioners.

Outlook

Brazil is making great strides on several fronts—economically, legislatively, and professionally. Largely through the strong advocacy efforts of high-profile library associations and library leaders, their work is coming to fruition. Their older vanguard librarians are also mentoring younger colleagues for leadership. Brazil's two greatest challenges for the future will be the continuing disparity between the haves and have-nots (which impacts both physical and intellectual access to information), and the ability to sustain the progress of school librarians and librarians in general. Brazil's school librarians have the intellectual capacity to develop federated collections, services, and training, largely facilitated through technology, which will show that the country's trust and investment in them is justified. Ideally, social media can support collaboration and collective intelligence across the nation.

The International School Library Future

Drawing from the current situations and future hopes for the school libraries in all three nations, what will the International Library 2025 look like? Factors both inside and outside each country, as well as the profession, determine what the future holds for their school librarians. Political-economic stability and growth and continued advances in technology can improve the infrastructure to expand access to information. Increased globalization and social media can lead to more available information, often generated collectively, for school library access and school librarian training.

No one path exists for developing school libraries, but rather school librarians need to leverage the socio-politico-cultural aspects of their countries to advance the profession and its services. The three nations described in this chapter vary significantly in terms of culture, literacy rates, infrastructure, and library quality. Each developing nation pictures school libraries differently, which drives their future direction. In Nepal the focus can be on local resources and artistic expression; in Honduras digital services are a high priority; and in Brazil school libraries often join public libraries, providing academic and recreational support. Table 8.1 provides a statistical comparison among the three countries and the United States that illustrates the variations among school libraries across the globe (Central Intelligence Agency 2012).

As noted previously, Brazil has the most stable government, the most resources, and the greatest number of people. The new president seems to be a solid choice, and Brazil has been in the vanguard of initiatives such as self-support and green technology. The recent push for joint community libraries may help address the digital divide and the mandate for school libraries and librarians. On the other hand, Nepal and Honduras may continue to struggle with unstable governments and rely on outside help, although both countries seem to want to improve conditions through their own efforts

Table 8.1. Statistical Comparison of the United States and Nepal, Honduras, and Brazil

	United States	Brazil	Honduras	Nepal
Population (in millions)	1,343	205.7	8.3	29.9
Literacy rate	99%	88%	80%	49%
New book titles published per year	328,259	18,712	290	NA
GDP per capita	$48,100	$11,600	$4,300	$1,300
Internet hosts	498,000,000	23,790,000	27,074	41,532
Electricity consumption (in billion KWH)	3,741	455.7	6.5	4.8

as well. Improved access to digital information may set the stage for such self-development.

While it is important to acknowledge the differences implicit in libraries found in different nations, a study of their challenges and needs reveals some common themes. School libraries in these three countries are representative of many developing countries, which face issues that challenge them more than further-developed nations. Fortunately, all three countries share some common promising factors that have been shown to predict successful school librarians: strong librarian leaders, strong library associations, strong partners or stakeholders, collaboration with other types of librarians, and commitment to librarian training (Farmer 2008).

Challenges

Many developing countries have high illiteracy rates and low gross national products. Nepal, Brazil, and Honduras all have strong oral and visual traditions rather than written ones. Music and crafts are popular in these countries, but museums are not. While creative expression is valued, archives are not as important because the emphasis is on the present rather than the long term. As a result, we find the lack of a reading culture. For publishing to flourish, there must be a sizable population of readers with disposable incomes, so local school libraries suffer from a paucity of local and national publishing.

Often the government infrastructure for schools and libraries, which would be significant stockers of publications, is underfunded or lacks capacity. Competent writers are more likely to get educated and published abroad.

These nations are additionally challenged by uneven electricity and other public utilities necessary for an established technology infrastructure. In some cases, governments are unstable or have little revenue to support public utilities, which are needed to operate libraries. In other cases, the country's terrain or climate hinders construction and delivery of such service; for instance, mountains are obvious barriers in Nepal and jungles impede communication in Brazil and Honduras.

A final common theme is underdeveloped or nonexistent professional training in library science. Some countries have very low education levels; furthermore, library science is not always valued in comparison with other professions such as health care and business. Some countries like Honduras have no formal library science program at the university level, which forces prospective librarians to seek their education in other countries and requires substantial personal expense. Nepal has no school library track in its librarianship academic training, and Brazil has only started such a track in the past five years.

Solutions for the International School Library

Despite the challenges described above, several strategies can help these countries overcome their existing limitations or constraints. First, the provision of low-cost computers and smartphones powered by alternative energy (e.g., solar or manual) will improve circumstances for school libraries. The three countries all have active cell phone businesses, and information can be produced and disseminated digitally. International satellite Internet connectivity would empower countries to improve communications without constructing labor-intensive physical lines across the land.

The local production of information resources is a critical strategy to address collection development restraints. With free and low-cost social media, students and other members of the public can generate and disseminate digital information that librarians can then collect, organize, and offer for public access. In the area of library education, globalization can assist efforts to improve library science professional development. Preservice librarians can gain access to library science courses virtually from any place that has Internet connectivity.

Government stability and priorities, economic capacity, land features, communication infrastructure, educational situations, literacy practices, and cultural traditions all impact the current school library situation, and are likely predictors of conditions that future school libraries have to address (UNESCO 2003). On the other hand, the intellectual capacity and resourcefulness of dedicated school librarians who are responsive to their communities can override these external obstacles.

The Ideal Future

In the best-case scenario for 2025, every school will have a tech-savvy, trained school librarian who manages a busy learning commons, often alongside librarians with specialized expertise. The facility itself will provide spaces for different functions: cozy reading pods, study circles and genius bars for collaborative learning (a strong suit in these three countries), production space to support individual and collective knowledge generation, and an expression area for "live" and visual arts of all kinds. The library will be bustling as students collectively gather and generate knowledge to be uploaded to the online national (or international) community knowledge repository. It should be noted that while school libraries may exist within a school, along with other specialized libraries such as research centers, the concept of lifelong learning will lead to more fluid centers of learning such that formal and informal education will commingle in multitype community libraries. Different age groups will teach each other, be it cuisine, oral history, dance steps, alternative medicine, financial matters, or new technologies.

Libraries will likely have many different configurations, from high-tech specialized libraries to comprehensive small community public spaces, from mobile-based virtual libraries to interactive cultural centers. These libraries may be segmented by user type, by subject domain, or by function so that school libraries per se may be an amorphous concept. In fact, library configurations may be dynamic in nature, changing in response to changing needs. All types of libraries and their institutions will collaborate to provide seamless and relevant resources and services for their communities, and their affiliations may change from situation to situation as well.

The collection will include student and local documents and other cultural artifacts, some of which will be projected on moveable small-group screens and accessed through their portable learning devices. Part of the collection will encourage hands-on manipulation for creating clothing and crafts and the use of historical items such as typewriters and flash drives. Students will read more because they can read relevant materials that are created by their peers and local experts; they will also learn to read so they can learn to write, for example, song lyrics, local history, job applications, graphic novels, video scripts, technical guides, and many other publications. The community nature of libraries will facilitate cross-generational reading. Furthermore, students will understand that the concept of literacy extends beyond the written word to encompass visual, audio, and other media.

Technology will continue to drive library services. The school community will be able to use solar- and hand-powered mobile devices to access, create, and share information worldwide. Through the online networked repository, communities will be able to access each other's materials. Students and other library users will be able to collaborate across the world on green educational technology projects. The community will also access "cybrarian" specialists from around the world through online conferencing.

School librarians will be trained in several steps: basic training on resource management, education, technology and communication that incorporates face-to-face sessions, Skype (or its successors), and downloaded materials. Advanced and specialized online modules will provide training for area school library leaders, and just-in-time training will be available online from a directory of school library training centers. School librarians will form learning communities to develop interest-based expertise and produce digital products for their constituents. They will also teach their colleagues and develop shared databases of instructional materials. In all circumstances, librarians will work together for permanent and enforced legislation and financial support of libraries in-country. Considering their shared heritages, it is likely that Honduran librarians will join with their Central American neighbors to develop an international library system. In other countries, international collaboration may be more short term, depending on the need.

Getting to the International School Library 2025

The ideal conditions described above require that the government and the general public in each nation begin to value school libraries (UNESCO 2003). School librarians will need to advocate more effectively in light of country priorities and the misconception that everything is free and available on the Internet. It should be noted that digital citizenship has become more important these days, partly because the public has witnessed more cybercrime and online dangers to youth. School librarians have the expertise to instruct students in safe and responsible technology use, so they would be wise to leverage this in their favor. The Internet also signals warnings about the devaluation of reading, and school librarians need to show how a variety of literacies are required and how the school library can collect these resources and instruct students in their effective use. Indeed, school librarians have to reeducate the public and themselves as to the nature of school libraries, including the resources they provide and how to access them, their instructional role, and the nature of literacies. If, on the other hand, school librarians do not proactively take charge and remain at the vanguard of changing needs, school libraries and school librarians could disappear.

School librarians need to work closely with their communities to assess local needs and interests as well as available resources. It will be important for them to take leadership roles by identifying what local resources need to be developed and then collecting, organizing, and making these resources available as part of the library's collection. In addition to providing physical access to the collection, school librarians need to work with educators and with users to integrate literacies (e.g., reading, technology, information, and cultural) into teaching and learning. This role necessitates librarianship preparation programs that address literacies and educational issues as part of their curriculum. Librarians can also forward the idea of education as helping learners to appreciate and express their cultures accurately and authentically. Finally, they will need to develop and advance school librarian and library standards as well as professional development opportunities to support those standards (American Association of School Librarians 2009; American Library Association 2009).

These external and internal factors constitute key preconditions for school library sustainability (Farmer 2008). The burden for success, though, lies in the hands of current and future school librarians. By leveraging their cultural assets, school librarians can optimize their own value as they provide relevant information that will prepare students to contribute to their culture as well as to the information society as a whole. The International Library 2025 will be a result of school librarians' ability to gauge and take advantage of political and economic situations to address the needs of their school communities, and to work collaboratively across their countries to deliver the resources and services needed in the future.

References

American Association of School Librarians. 2009. *Empowering Learners: Guidelines for School Library Programs*. Chicago: American Library Association.

American Library Association. 2009. *Core Competencies of Librarianship*. Chicago: American Library Association.

Campello, Bernadete. 2009. "Developing Students' Information Skills in Brazilian School Libraries: The Librarian's Role." *School Libraries Worldwide* 15, no. 1: 14–28.

Central Intelligence Agency. 2012. *World Factbook*. Washington, DC: Central Intelligence Agency.

Farmer, Lesley. 2008. "Predictors for Success: Experiences of Beginning and Expert Teacher Librarians." In *Educational Media and Technology Annual*, edited by V. J. McClendon, 157–84. Westport, CT: Libraries Unlimited.

International Federation of Library Associations. 1999. *IFLA/UNESCO School Library Manifesto*. The Hague, Netherlands: International Federation of Library Associations.

———. 2002. *School Library Guidelines*. The Hague, Netherlands: International Federation of Library Associations.

National Pedagogical University Francisco Morazan. 2011. *Plan of Graduate Studies in Library Science Master's Degree*. Tegucigalpa, Honduras: National Pedagogical University Francisco Morazan.

UNESCO. 2003. *Building the Information Society: A Global Challenge in the New Millennium*. Geneva, Switzerland: UNESCO. http://portal.unesco.org/ci/en/files/25347/11895190701DPGeneva_en.pdf/DPGeneva_en.pdf.

REDESIGNING LIBRARY SERVICES

A Manifesto (Abridged)

Michael Buckland

Introduction

The central purpose of libraries is to provide a service: access to information.

The good news is that additional, different means for providing library service are becoming available in a manner unprecedented since the nineteenth century. The challenge for all concerned with libraries is to determine how, whether, and when these new means should be used.

Much has been written in recent years on the possible impact of new technology on "the library of the future." This is nothing new. It could be that long-term visions have a beneficial effect in stimulating debate and thought. However one may suspect that little of the rhetoric and few of the specific technological proposals have been of much direct help to those with the heavy responsibility of planning for the future of any particular library. The problems of existing libraries are severe. Visions of electronic libraries seem uncertain and suspect. Even if such a vision seems good, it is not at all clear that plausible paths of development from here to there have been adequately mapped.

Redesigning Library Services has been written on three assumptions:

1. There has been insufficient attention to *strategic* planning, that is, the making of decisions relative to a three to ten year time frame.

2. A disproportionate amount of attention has been paid to new information technology.

3. There is, in fact, considerable experience on which our strategic planning can be based, more than is generally realized.

Suppose that one were charged with making recommendations concerning the development of a library service over a three to ten year range, what sort of conclusions might one be justified in reaching? The purpose of this book is to suggest some general bases for planning or, at least, to provide a general framework for thinking about future library services.

The purpose being pursued in library service is the provision of access to books, journals, and other informative materials. Libraries have never had a monopoly since much of what is in demand is also available in personal collections, bookshops, from personal contacts, and, indeed, from other sorts of libraries. However, even if it is not a monopoly, it is clearly the major role and niche of library service. Now, in addition to the customary difficulties in providing library service, the radical changes in the technology available as *means* for providing service leaves the future unclear.

In such a situation we need to be prepared to retreat to first principles. Library service is a busy, service-oriented activity, with a deeply-rooted emphasis, reflected in the professional literature, on practical and technical matters, on means, rather than on ends, and tactics rather than strategy. Nevertheless, there is currently a healthy awareness that major changes are likely and a recognition, for example, of some convergence between library services, computing services, and telecommunications services, of probable changes in the publishing world, and that library management is, at least in part, concerned as much with the management of service as with the management of books.

Three Types of Library

The following three types of library provision, based on the technology used, provide a convenient framework for discussing future library service.

Until recently libraries' technical operations (e.g., purchasing, processing, cataloging, and circulation) and library materials (primarily texts) were both based on paper and cardboard: We call this the "Paper Library." Strictly speaking, libraries have always included materials other than paper such as clay tablets, vellum, film, and so on, but these other media make little difference for our present purposes.

Over the past two decades, libraries' technical operations have become based on computer technology while the library's materials still remain overwhelmingly on paper and paper-like media: The "Automated Library."

The prospect that library *materials*, as well as library operations, will increasingly be in electronic form indicates a further change in the means of library service: The "Electronic Library." See Table A.1.

Table A.1. Technological Bases of Library Operations and Materials

	Technical Operations	*Library Materials*
Paper Library	Paper	Paper
Automated Library	Computer	Paper
Electronic Library	Computer	Electronic media

The concept of the Electronic Library is important because library *materials* will increasingly be available in machine-readable form, users will need access to them, and *access will, therefore, have to be provided.* One can speculate about the eventual balance between paper materials and electronic materials or, if one wishes, on the prospects for paperless libraries, but these issues are of little significance compared with the underlying assumption that arrangements for access to some materials in electronic form will have to be provided. Today libraries are, or are becoming, Automated Libraries, with the imminent prospect of needing to evolve, at least in part, into Electronic Libraries. Since paper documents (and other nonelectronic media such as film) seem unlikely to disappear, we may expect the Automated Library and the Electronic Library to co-exist indefinitely. More specifically, we can expect, and should plan for, any real library service to be a blend: part Automated Library and part Electronic Library.

It seems that the relative stability of the past century is but a prologue to another period of radical change, comparable in significance to that of the late nineteenth century with its exciting renaissance of ideas and techniques. This time change is enabled less by new ideas than by a change in the underlying technology, which is all the more reason to reassess our assumptions about future libraries. As operations and services become more complex and more capital-intensive, ad hoc, unsystematic decision-making can lead library services down unproductive paths. Correcting mistakes becomes expensive and disruptive.

Creative planning needs to be central, because of the superiority of planning over merely reacting to events. We—funders, providers, and users of library services—need to reflect creatively on what we do and why. Planning offers us a chance to create the future.

The Paper Library

Library services as we know them best are based on the technology of paper. Card, as in card catalogs, is but a stiff form of paper. Libraries' technical operations are steadily being computerized and, thereby, paper libraries are now being transformed into what we are calling Automated Libraries. The Paper Library proved effective and durable for an extended period. Nevertheless, the serious limitations of the Paper Library need to be reviewed explicitly if we are to make an informed and balanced appraisal of the other options, the Automated Library and the Electronic Library.

1. Paper is a strictly localized medium. It and the user must be in the same place at the same time.

2. A single paper document can, in general, only be used by one person at a time.

3. Paper copies of documents can be made by reprinting and by photographic and more modern reprographic means, but the same limitations apply to a copy as to the original.

4. Paper as a medium is rather inflexible. Paper documents really do not lend themselves to being merged, divided, reformatted, and restored to earlier versions.

5. Collections on paper become bulky and create storage problems.

The localness of paper documents remains an unsolved constraint. A consequence is that each library collection is more or less skillfully selected to match the needs of those using it, which is a great advantage over finding oneself in a vast warehouse of indiscriminately assembled materials, whether paper or electronic.

Librarians and library users have long wished for rapidly-available, inexpensive facsimiles. Television was promptly recognized, at least as early as 1925, as demonstrating the potential of electronic telecommunications for remote access to library materials. "But what a revolution for information retrieval and especially for libraries television can bring," exclaimed the German librarian Walter Schürmeyer in 1935. "Perhaps one day we will see our reading rooms deserted and in their place a room without people in which books requested by telephone are displayed, which the users read in their homes using television."

The Automated Library

We use *Automated Library* to denote a library in which the collections of library materials are primarily on paper but in which the library's *procedures* have been computerized. Libraries are very record-intensive: Not only is each title different but, for many purposes, the records needed for library operations must necessarily be very concerned with *individual copies* of each title. A circulation system must know precisely *which* copy of *which* volume of *which* edition of *which* title was borrowed by precisely *which* borrower and *when* it is due back. Considerations of service, of cost, and of the humane use of staff all argue for the use of computers to ease the burden and to increase the effectiveness of handling library records.

Bringing order to chaos and achieving collaboration both depend on shared understanding: on standards. Library service has long depended on shared standards, of which the adoption of standardized cataloging codes and standardized subject classification schemes are two very important examples. These two examples and most library standards may facilitate automation and make computerized procedures more cost-effective, but they have little to do with computers directly.

The sensible alternative, for anyone interested in using computers, was to try to keep the advantages and to delegate the inconvenience. Instead of withdrawing from one's local on-line catalog in order to use another, one would prefer to command the local on-line catalog to extend the search to other on-line catalogs elsewhere on one's behalf and to retrieve and to present the results.

Experience with Library Automation

Paper Libraries of any size now either are or are becoming Automated Libraries. We have some familiarity with what is involved. In brief, the change from the nineteenth century design of the Paper Library to the Automated Library has been characterized by:

- standardization of data,
- remote access to files,
- the linking and combining of files,
- access to numerous different files from the same terminal,
- increased cooperative use of shared files,
- discontinuation of numerous, more-or-less duplicative local files,
- greater capability for doing things to and with the (computer-based) files, and
- increased vulnerability to technological failure.

The Automated Library perpetuates some of the problems of the Paper Library noted in the previous chapter. Because the collections of documents are still on paper, a localized medium, the need for local collections, the space needed for paper documents, the inflexibility of paper documents, the separation of documents from the users, opening hours for the collections (though no longer for the catalog), and competition for use of copies of documents all remain as much a problem in the Automated Library as in the Paper Library. The catalog may be used in a number of places. In particular, with remote access to the on-line catalog, the user is no longer separated from the catalog and the separation of catalog and documents is somewhat diminished since, on-line, a catalog can at long last be used in the bookstacks.

The Automated Library represents a significant improvement but for only some of the problems and, aside for the on-line catalog, benefits directly those who are *providing* the service rather than those who are *using* the service.

The Electronic Library

We use the term "Electronic Library" to describe the situation in which documents are stored in electronic form, rather than on paper or other localized media. Note that paper copies of electronic documents, or of excerpts from them, can generally be produced for the reader's convenience. However, the essence of the Electronic Library is that documents are stored and can be used in electronic (or similarly machine-readable) form.

The adoption of computers for libraries' technical operations, the transition from the Paper Library to the Automated Library, can be viewed as an evolutionary development. Much of the change represented, at least initially, the mechanization of previously manual procedures of the Paper Library. The changes have been, at least until the provision of on-line catalogs, mainly for internal efficiency and for the convenience of library employees. In contrast, the rise of the Electronic Library, in which materials are stored in electronic form, may seem more revolutionary than evolutionary because of the implications for the provision and use of library services. But is it really so radical a change? Where are the impacts on the provision of library service? How are we to achieve a graceful and efficient continuity of service as electronic documents come into use?

The Increase of Electronic Documents

The most obvious source of electronic documents is new publications issued in electronic form. But what of the older materials on paper that occupy so many miles of libraries' shelves? Libraries have undertaken a major, systematic effort at the retrospective conversion of older catalog records from cards to electronic records. What of the retrospective conversion of the texts of older paper documents themselves? The idea might seem wildly unrealistic, but there are grounds to believe that, over time, significant and increasing amounts of older material will become available as electronic documents. In selected areas, notably literature, texts have been converted for research purposes: All classical Greek texts and increasing quantities of medieval and modern literary texts are already available in electronic form. Devices have been available for some years that can scan printed material, derive digital versions, and "read" the text out loud for the blind and visually-impaired. The same approach can be used to convert paper texts into electronic form as an alternative to keying them when an electronic form of the text is needed for word processing purposes. These electronic copies are usually discarded or, at least, are not made systematically available. They could be.

Reinventing the Library

What are we to do with a document in electronic form? There is little choice but to do the same as we do with a paper document or with a microfilm document:

- Catalog it and, as with manuscripts, pay careful attention to which version or state of text it is.
- Store it in some accessible place.
- Give it a call number.
- Ensure that pertinent bibliographic and location data are accessible in or through bibliographic databases.

There seems no real alternative. Given that electronic documents exist and are becoming progressively more important, to ignore them would be to provide a progressively less complete library service. A library administration might choose to retain an exclusive concentration on paper, microfilm, and other localized media, but that would mean that access to electronic documents would have to be found through other channels, such as the computer center. The result would be a split in the provision of library service: the "library" providing access to only some kinds of documents; and another organization providing the balance of the library service—that which involves access to electronic documents.

The significant difference with an electronic document is that if you have the call number it should in principle be possible, from any workstation, to gain access to it remotely, view it, download it, and, in brief, "use" it. Think how much simpler and quicker it would be if librarians and, even better, library users could obtain their own interlibrary "loans" (now, technically, copies or excerpts) on a self-service basis, requiring the tolerance but not the time or energy of the staff of the library from which it is obtained. This change would be rather like the change from having closed library stacks, in which library employees had to fetch each book for users, to open stacks in which library users could obtain and examine books by themselves. Similarly, in the Electronic Library, library staff would be mainly concerned with creating and sustaining the system so that users could serve themselves.

Self-service, however, is a mixed blessing. It also assumes standardized, intelligible procedures, presupposes some expertise on the users' part, and may make it less easy for the service providers to know what is going well and what is not going well. Yet it may be the only affordable way to support large-scale library use.

The Architecture of the Electronic Library

What would it take to build an Electronic Library and, indeed, to make Electronic Library service common practice? To develop a library with electronic documents we do not appear to need to draw on anything in librarianship that is different from existing principles. Rather, as with paper and with microform, we have to interpret the same familiar principles in ways appropriate to the technical characteristics of the medium. With electronic documents, even more than with microforms, adherence to standards is important for progress. Electronic documents should themselves be in standard formats. Standards are needed for cataloging electronic documents. Communications formats are needed for conveying electronic documents. Substantial and compatible telecommunications protocols are of great importance. Much work needs to be done in developing and adopting compatible national and international standards for characters, images, documents, telecommunications, and so on.

The key to consideration of the Electronic Library is recognition that providing access to electronic documents will be needed. How the balance between paper and electronic documents will evolve is an interesting but less urgent issue.

Organization and Implementation

Good planning is a process that leads to consistent anticipatory decision making. Planning that does not influence decisions is futile. Decision making should be anticipatory in that plans should be ready for events as (or before) events occur. Decisions should be consistent with the mission of the organization and with each other. Bad planning or, more commonly, an absence of planning is reflected in decisions that are taken too late and that are inconsistent: Any good resulting from one decision is liable to be undone by the next.

With technological change there is often unfortunate confusion between "research and development" and "innovation." Research and development have to do with the *identification* of feasible new options and is a matter of inquiry, investigation, and testing. Innovation is a matter of selecting or rejecting available options and is a management activity. These are quite different activities. Failure to recognize the difference between them leads to the development of options that are not properly considered or to the adoption of impractical or unsuitable innovations.

The management of research and development, the implementation of change, and effective planning are important and widely underestimated skills. There is a large and useful literature on planning upon which one can draw.

The Challenge

The mission of library service is to support the purposes of the group to be served. The role of library service is to provide access to documents. We could, if we wished, choose to define documents generously to include a range of informative objects that can be stored and retrieved, not only writings and not only published writings.

Library service may be concerned with knowledge, but it is so in a fashion that is doubly indirect. Firstly, library services are concerned with texts and images that are representations of knowledge. Secondly, library services are, in practice, often concerned less with the texts and images themselves than with physical objects that are text-bearing and image-bearing, such as books, journals, manuscripts, and photographs. Libraries deal with text-bearing and image-bearing objects in vast quantities. Much of libraries' operating budgets and space is devoted not to the *use* of these materials, but to *assembling, organizing, and describing* these materials so that it would become possible to use them. Hence, any significant change in the technology of text-bearing objects or of handling them could have very profound consequences, not on the purpose and mission of library services, but on the means for achieving them.

Information technology may only be a means and not an end, but that does not make it unimportant. In the provision of library service a very large proportion of present budgets is devoted to arranging the means to enable service to be provided. The substitution of computing power, electronic data storage, and use of telecommunications holds considerable potential, not least because of the expectation that they will continue to become more attractive on cost grounds. The important questions become how and when the substitution of procedures based on new information technology should be adopted. The constraints include our limited ability to determine how to achieve that substitution, when that substitution will become cost-effective, and, at least as important, how to discriminate between substitutions that support improved library service and substitutions that subvert the mission and role of library service.

Beyond Substitution

The initial task can reasonably be to find out how and when to substitute techniques using new information technology in the place of more traditional methods. This, in itself, misjudges the real options. Each technology offers a different set of constraints. Each technology is suited for doing *different* things. The automating of manual procedures may well be worthwhile, but, in the longer term, misses the point of technological change. The initial question may be: How could library services be advantageously automated? This is a matter of doing the *same* things better. The longer term, more interesting question is: How could library service be re-designed with a change in technology? This is a matter of *how* to do better, *different* things.

Critical for addressing the second question—which better, different things should be done—is an understanding of past constraints upon library services that are attributable to the constraints of the technology of paper, card, and microform. However, constraints that are familiar tend to be transparent and not easy to recognize.

In "The Paper Library," we noted the constraints of paper. Paper is a strictly localized medium; a paper document is generally suited for use by only one person at a time; paper copies of paper documents have the same constraints as do the original; paper records are rather inflexible and can become expensively bulky. Computer-based processing and electronic document storage have been found to have their own distinctive characteristics. The constraints include a greater need for standardization, increased technical complexity, and greater dependence on equipment that is much more fragile and much more prone to obsolescence than that of a Paper Library.

Advantages of the new technology are that repetitive, mechanical tasks can be delegated to the machinery; the rate of increase in labor costs can thereby be moderated; electronic records can be modified, rearranged, and combined with each other; and, with telecommunications, distance becomes substantially irrelevant. These factors transform those aspects of library service that derive from the constraints of paper and cardboard. The location of the user, the catalog record, the bibliography, and the document cease to be dominating considerations. The user, the catalog, the bibliography, and the document can now be connected in ways that, hitherto, could only be dreamed about. As these changed constraints come to be appreciated it becomes clear that these new circumstances offer the possibility—indeed the inevitability— of new designs for library service.

Several major changes are indicated:

1. Since library materials in electronic form lend themselves to remote access and shared use, the assembling of local collections becomes less important. Coordinated collection development and cooperative, shared access to collections become more important.

2. With materials on paper, having copies stored locally is a necessary (though not a sufficient) condition for convenient access. With electronic materials, local storage may be desirable but is no longer necessary.

3. In the meanwhile, those to be served are changing their information-handling habits. Paper and pen are being supplemented by desk-top workstations, capable of using a multiplicity of remote sources. This leads to an entirely different perspective: from a library-centered world view to one that is user-centered.

4. These technological changes also invite reconsideration of the professional orthodoxy of consolidating academic library services. The view that a multiplicity of branch and departmental libraries is inefficient might well change.

5. The functions of the library, the computer center, and the telecommunications office are converging, overlapping, or, at least, more closely related. New patterns are evolving in the relationships between libraries, publishers, and others in the information industry. The roles of archives, libraries, museums, and other information stores seem likely to become less clearly differentiated.

6. There is much greater opportunity to bring service to wherever potential users of library service happen to be.

Catalogs, collections, buildings, and library staff are the familiar means for providing library services. Computers, networks, and electronic documents provide additional means with interesting possibilities.

Hitherto library services have been dominated by local catalogs, local collections, and great inequalities in the geographical distribution of services. The constraints on library service are changing right now. None of this is an argument for abandoning paper and local collections. All of this requires us to think again about the mission of the library, the role of library, and the means of providing service. For the first time in one hundred years we face the grand and difficult challenge of redesigning library services.

Author's Note

Redesigning Library Services: A Manifesto was originally published in 1992 by the American Library Association. The full text is available at http://sunsite .berkeley.edu/Literature/Library/Redesigning/html.html.

About the Contributors

Brett Bonfield is director of the Collingswood (NJ) Public Library. Bonfield is co-founder and editor at *In the Library with the Lead Pipe* and a 2012 *Library Journal* Mover and Shaker. He graduated from Drexel University's iSchool in 2007. Among a wide variety of roles in the American Library Association, he served as chair of the Future Perfect Presidential Task Force in 2010–2011 and was a member of the Young Librarians Task Force. He spent two years as treasurer of the New Jersey Library Association and now serves on the board of the New Jersey Council for the Humanities.

John Chrastka is the founder of EveryLibrary, a political action committee, and a partner in AssociaDirect, a Chicago-based consultancy focused on supporting associations in membership recruitment, conference, and governance activities. He serves as president of the board of trustees for the Berwyn (IL) Public Library and is a former president of the Reaching Across Illinois Libraries System (RAILS) multitype library system. Prior to his work at AssociaDirect, he was director for membership development at the American Library Association. He is a current trustee member of ALA and the Illinois Library Association.

Lesley Farmer, professor at California State University–Long Beach, coordinates the Librarianship program. Dr. Farmer has worked as a library media teacher in K–12 school settings as well as in public, special, and academic libraries. She serves as vice president of association relations for the International Association for School Librarianship and as chair for the Education Division of Special Libraries Association and edits the IFLA School Libraries and Resource Centers Section newsletter. Dr. Farmer is a frequent presenter and writer for the profession. Her latest books include *Using Qualitative Methods in Action Research* (with Doug Cook, ALA 2011), *Youth-Serving Libraries in Japan, Russia, and the United States* (Scarecrow Press 2012), and *Instructional Design for Librarians and Information Professionals* (Neal-Schuman 2012).

Dave Harmeyer is professor and associate dean of university libraries at Azusa Pacific University (APU). He teaches in the online teacher-librarian credential/master's program and is known for taking his students into the 3D immersive environment Second Life. In 2007 he completed a doctorate in educational technology at Pepperdine University where he defended an award-winning dissertation, *Online Virtual Chat Library*

Reference Service: A Quantitative and Qualitative Analysis. Harmeyer is a column editor and writer for *The Reference Librarian* and is on the board for the *Journal of Religious and Theological Information*. Prior to joining APU in 1997, he directed the library at the International School of Theology in San Bernardino, California. He and his wife have two daughters and reside in Southern California.

Megan Hodge earned her Master of Science in Library Science from the University of North Texas in 2010 and is a teaching and learning librarian for Virginia Commonwealth University. She is also the vice-president/president-elect for the ALA New Members Round Table. In 2011 she was an ALA Emerging Leader and co-founded the Virginia Library Association New Members Round Table. Her professional interests are library human resources, young adult services, and instructional design.

Ben Malczewski is the Humanities Department Manager for the Toledo-Lucas County Public Library and lives in Ann Arbor, Michigan. He attended the University of Toledo, the University of Edinburgh, and Wayne State University, and his background is in literary criticism and film studies. Before entering librarianship he was an Americorps volunteer and social worker in the Pacific Northwest. His freelance writing appears frequently in *Library Journal* (among others), where he primarily covers media market analytics and projection as well as emerging technologies.

Krisellen Maloney has been the dean of libraries at the University of Texas at San Antonio since 2009. Her previous roles included associate university librarian for digital services and technology planning at Georgetown University, director of information technology in the Library of Congress Law Library, and team leader of digital library and information systems at University of Arizona Libraries. Maloney holds a PhD in information science, an MA in library science, and MS and bachelor's degrees in management information systems, all from the University of Arizona.

Hugh Rundle has worked in public libraries since 2001 and holds a Graduate Diploma in Information Management from RMIT University. He has worked in systems, youth, and reference services and is currently Information Management and Kew Librarian at the City of Boroondara Library Service in Melbourne, Australia. Hugh joined *In the Library with the Lead Pipe* as an author/editor in 2013, blogs about libraries at http://hughrundle.net, and can be found on Twitter at @hughrundle.

Index

Note: The letter *t* indicates that the entry refers to a page's table.